Show me

WordPerfect® 6 for Windows™
A Visual Guide to the Basics

Sherry Kinkoph

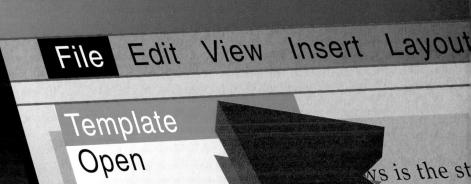

a

alpha
books

A Division of Prentice Hall Computer Publishing
201 W. 103rd Street, Indianapolis, IN 46290

File   Edit   View   Insert   Layout

Template
Open
Close

Save
Save As...

QuickFinder
Master Document
Compare Document
Document Summary

DEDICATION

To my grandparents—Mima and Carl Willard, Fay and Lavern Williams.

International Standard Book Number: 1-56761-299-7
Library of Congress Catalog Card Number: 93-71737

96 95 94 93   8 7 6 5 4 3 2 1

Interpretation of the printing code: the rightmost number of the first series of numbers is the year of the book's printing; the rightmost number of the second series of numbers is the number of the book's printing. For example, a printing code of 93-1 shows that the first printing of the book occurred in 1993.

Screen reproductions in this book were created by means of the program Collage Plus from Inner Media, Inc., Hollis, NH.

Printed in the United States of America by
Shepard Poorman Communications Corp.
7301 North Woodland Drive, Indianapolis, IN 46278

TRADEMARKS

Publisher

Marie Butler-Knight

Associate Publisher

Lisa A. Bucki

Managing Editor

Elizabeth Keaffaber

Development Editor

Seta Frantz

Manuscript Editor

Barry Childs-Helton

Cover Designer

Scott Fullmer

Production Team

*Diana Bigham, Tim Cox, Howard Jones,
Roger Morgan, Beth Rago, Greg Simsic*

*Special thanks to Kelly Oliver for ensuring the
technical accuracy of this book.*

CONTENTS

Part 3 Enhancing Your Document 73

Glossary 107

Installing WordPerfect for Windows 6.0 111

Index 113

INTRODUCTION

Have you ever said to yourself, "I wish someone would just *show me* how to use WordPerfect for Windows." If you have, this *Show Me* book is for you. In it, you won't find detailed explanations of what's going on in your computer each time you enter a command. Instead, you will see pictures that *show you*, step by step, how to perform a particular task.

This book will make you feel as though you have your very own personal trainer standing next to you, pointing at the screen and showing you exactly what to do.

WHAT IS WORDPERFECT FOR WINDOWS?

WordPerfect for Windows is a *word processing program* used to create letters, memos, reports, manuscripts, and more. Any document that requires words can be created with WordPerfect for Windows. That includes anything from a one-page list to a 600-page book.

With WordPerfect for Windows, you can easily:

- Create documents and print out as many copies as you like.
- Check for spelling and grammatical errors with WordPerfect's spell checker and grammar checker.
- Make changes to text, such as copying it and moving it, inserting new text, or deleting text you don't want. (This is called *editing*.)
- Make changes in the style and size of your text, such as making characters bolder and bigger. (This is called *formatting*.)
- Save all your work so you can use your document again.

These are just a few of WordPerfect's features.

What Does WordPerfect for Windows Look Like?

If you've worked with other Windows-based programs, you'll find a familiar look and feel with WordPerfect for Windows. The main screen where you create all of your documents looks just like a window. Text is typed in the open area; buttons, menus, and borders surround the edges of the screen, awaiting your commands.

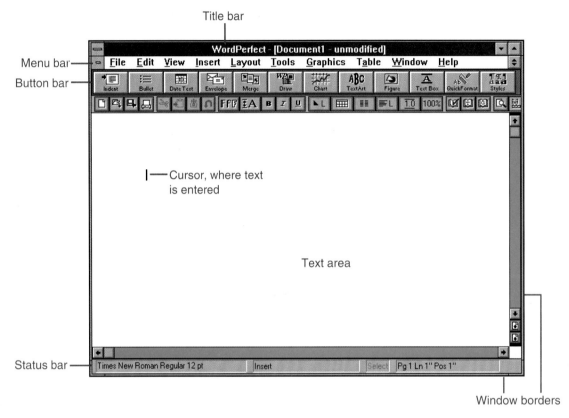

Feeling a bit intimidated? Don't worry, this book will show you all you need to know about working with WordPerfect for Windows!

HOW TO USE THIS BOOK

Using this book is as simple as falling off your chair. Just flip to the task that you want to perform, and follow the steps. You will see easy, step-by-step instructions that tell you which keys to press and which commands to select. You will also see step-by-step pictures that show you what to do. Follow the steps or the pictures (or both) to complete the task. Here's an example of a set of instructions from this book.

2

Saving a Document

1 Click on **F**ile, or press **Alt+F**.

2 Click on Save **A**s, or press **A**.

Numbered steps will correspond with the numbers shown on the figures.

3 Type the document name in the Filename box.

4 Select drive, directory, and file type options, if desired.

5 Click on **OK**, or press **Enter** when finished.

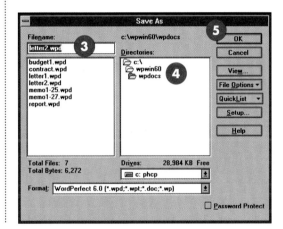

Every computer book has its own way of telling you which buttons to push and which keys to press. Here's how this book handles those formalities:

- Keys you should press appear as they do on your keyboard (for example, press **Alt** or press **F10**). If you need to press more than one key at once, the keys are separated with plus signs. For example, if the text tells you to press **Alt+F**, hold down the **Alt** key while pressing the **F** key.

- Text you should type is printed in **boldface type like this**.

- Some features are activated by selecting a menu and then a command. If I tell you to "select **F**ile **N**ew," you should open the **F**ile menu and select the **N**ew command. In this book, the selection letter is printed in boldface type for easy recognition.

Introduction

Definitions in Plain English

In addition to the basic step-by-step approach, pages may contain "Learning the Lingo" definitions to help you understand key terms. These definitions are placed off to the side, so you can easily skip them if you want to.

LEARNING THE LINGO

Pull-down menu: A menu that appears at the top of the screen, listing various commands. The menu is not visible until you select it from the menu bar. The menu then drops down, covering a small part of the screen.

Quick Refreshers

If you need to know how to perform some other task in order to perform the current task, look for a Quick Refresher. With the Quick Refresher, you won't have to flip through the book to learn how to perform the other task; the information is right where you need it.

QUICK REFRESHER

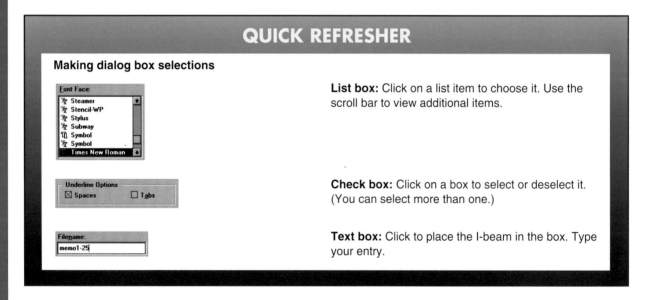

Making dialog box selections

List box: Click on a list item to choose it. Use the scroll bar to view additional items.

Check box: Click on a box to select or deselect it. (You can select more than one.)

Text box: Click to place the I-beam in the box. Type your entry.

Tips, Ideas, and Shortcuts

Throughout this book, you will encounter tips that provide important information about a task, or tell you how to perform the task more quickly.

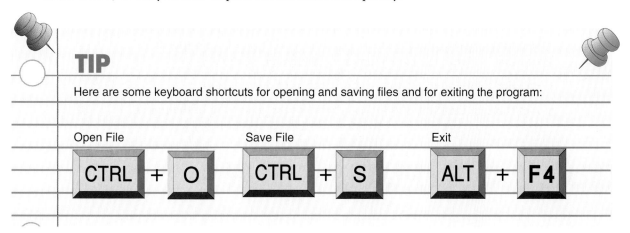

TIP

Here are some keyboard shortcuts for opening and saving files and for exiting the program:

| Open File | Save File | Exit |
| CTRL + O | CTRL + S | ALT + F4 |

Exercises

Because most people learn by doing, several exercises throughout the book give you additional practice performing a task.

To practice what you have learned about using menus from the menu bar, follow these steps:

1 Click on **View** from the menu bar, or press **Alt+V**.

2 Click on **B**utton Bar, or press **B**.

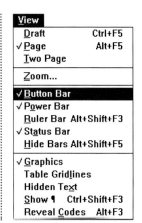

Where Should You Start?

If this is your first encounter with computers, read the next section, "Quick Computer Tour," before reading anything else. This section explains some computer basics that you need to know in order to get your computer up and running.

Once you know the basics, you can work through this book from beginning to end, or skip around from task to task, as needed. If you decide to skip around, there are several ways you can find what you're looking for:

- Use the Table of Contents at the front of this book to find a specific task you want to perform.

- Use the complete index at the back of this book to look up a specific task or topic, and find the page number on which it is covered.

- Use the color-coded sections to find groups of related tasks.

- Flip through the book and look at the task titles at the top of the pages. This method works best if you know the general location of the task in the book.

QUICK COMPUTER TOUR

If this is your first time in front of a computer, the next few sections will teach you the least you need to know to get started.

Parts of a Computer

Think of a computer as a car. The system unit holds the engine that powers the computer. The monitor is like the windshield that lets you see where you're going. And the keyboard and mouse are like the steering wheel, which allow you to control the computer.

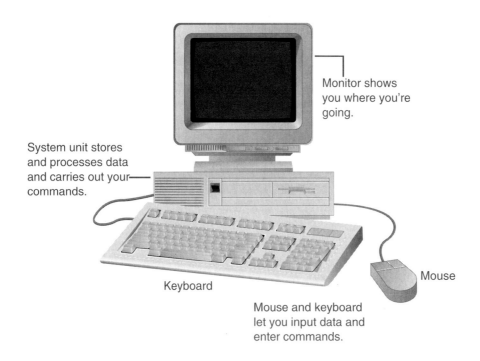

Monitor shows you where you're going.

System unit stores and processes data and carries out your commands.

Keyboard

Mouse

Mouse and keyboard let you input data and enter commands.

The System Unit

The system unit contains three basic elements. The *central processing unit* (CPU) does all the "thinking" for the computer. *Random-access memory* (RAM) stores instructions and data while the CPU is processing them. *Disk drives* store information permanently on disks to keep the information safe. At the back of the system unit, several *ports* allow you to connect other devices to it, such as a keyboard, mouse, and printer.

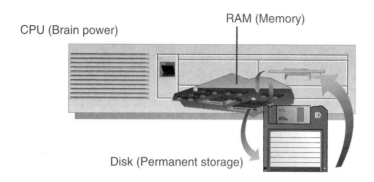

CPU (Brain power)

RAM (Memory)

Disk (Permanent storage)

Using a Keyboard

The keyboard is no mystery. It contains a set of *alphanumeric* (letter and number) keys for entering text, *arrow* keys for moving around on-screen, and *function* keys (F1, F2, and so on) for entering commands. It also has some odd keys, including *Alt* (Alternative), *Ctrl* (Control), and *Esc* (Escape) that perform special actions.

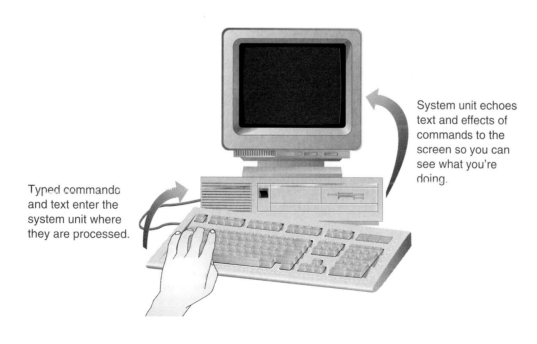

System unit echoes text and effects of commands to the screen so you can see what you're doing.

Typed commands and text enter the system unit where they are processed.

Using a Mouse

Like the keyboard, a mouse allows you to communicate with the computer. You roll the mouse around on your desk to move a *mouse pointer* on the screen. You can use the pointer to open menus and select other items on-screen. Here are some mouse techniques you must master:

Pointing. To point, roll the mouse on your desk until the tip of the mouse pointer is on the item to which you want to point on-screen.

Clicking. To click on an item, point to the desired item, and then hold the mouse steady while you press and release the mouse button. Use the left mouse button unless I tell you specifically to use the right button.

Double-clicking. To double-click, hold the mouse steady while you press and release the mouse button twice quickly.

Right-clicking. To right-click, click using the right mouse button instead of the left button.

Drag. To hold down the left mouse button and move the mouse to a new position.

Understanding Disks, Directories, and Files

Whatever you type (a letter, a list of names, a tax return) is stored only in your computer's temporary memory, and is erased when the electricity is turned off. To protect your work, you must *save* it in a *file* on a *disk*.

A *file* is like a folder that you might use to store a report or a letter. You name the file, so you can later find and retrieve the information it contains.

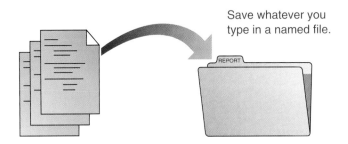

Save whatever you type in a named file.

REPORT

Files are stored on *disks*. Your computer probably has a *hard disk* inside it (called "drive C") to which you can save your files. You can also save files to *floppy disks*, which you insert into the slots (the floppy disk drives) on the front of the computer.

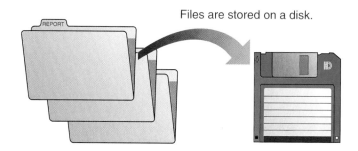

Files are stored on a disk.

To keep files organized on a disk, you can create *directories* on the disk. Each directory acts as a drawer in a filing cabinet, storing a group of related files. Although you can create directories on both floppy and hard disks, most people use directories only on hard disks.

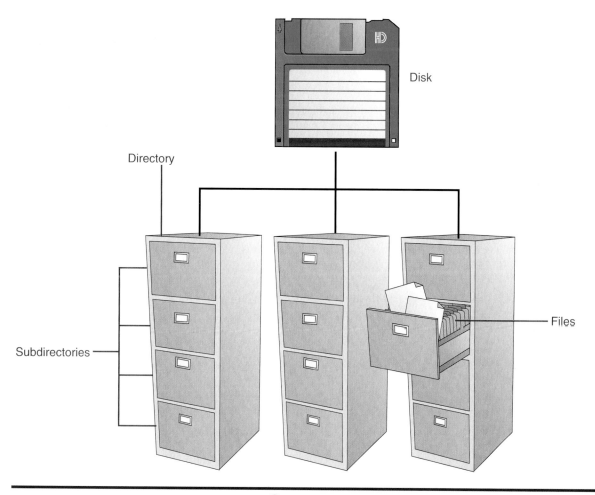

Disk

Directory

Subdirectories

Files

Introduction

PART 1

Basic WordPerfect for Windows Tasks

In this section, you'll learn how to accomplish basic WordPerfect for Windows tasks, such as starting and exiting. You'll familiarize yourself with the WordPerfect screen, and what it takes to navigate the program.

In this section, you'll learn about:

- Starting Windows
- Starting WordPerfect for Windows
- Understanding the WordPerfect Screen
- Using WordPerfect Menus
- Using Dialog Boxes
- Using the Power Bar
- Using the Button Bar
- Getting Help
- Exiting WordPerfect for Windows

STARTING WINDOWS

Why Start Windows?

The first procedure you'll need to know is how to start Windows. You cannot start WordPerfect for Windows 6.0 without first starting Windows and displaying the *Windows desktop* on your screen. Once Windows is up and running, you'll see the *Program Manager*, which is used to run other applications, such as WordPerfect for Windows.

Starting Windows

1 Make sure your computer and monitor are turned on, then at the DOS prompt (which looks like **C:>** or **C:\>**), type **win**.

2 Press **Enter**.

LEARNING THE LINGO

DOS Prompt: A set of characters on the left side of the screen, followed by a blinking underline. DOS commands are typed in at the DOS prompt.

Applications: Programs that run on your computer, such as word processing, or spreadsheet programs.

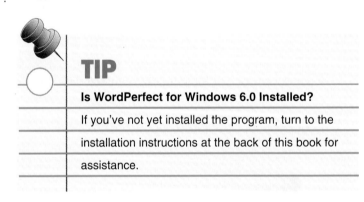

TIP

Is WordPerfect for Windows 6.0 Installed?

If you've not yet installed the program, turn to the installation instructions at the back of this book for assistance.

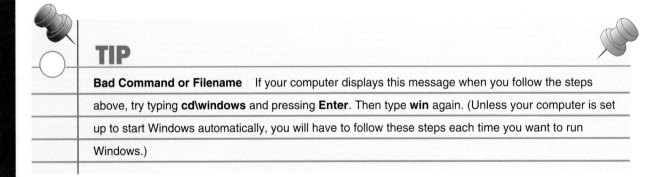

TIP

Bad Command or Filename If your computer displays this message when you follow the steps above, try typing **cd\windows** and pressing **Enter**. Then type **win** again. (Unless your computer is set up to start Windows automatically, you will have to follow these steps each time you want to run Windows.)

STARTING WORDPERFECT FOR WINDOWS

When to Start WordPerfect for Windows

Before you can begin creating documents with WordPerfect for Windows 6.0, you must first learn the steps for starting the program from the Windows Program Manager screen.

The Program Manager screen is the first screen displayed when you start Windows. Locate the WordPerfect for Windows *group icon*, a small picture with the label "WPWin 6.0" below it. This icon represents the WordPerfect program group. Once opened, you'll see the WordPerfect *program group window*.

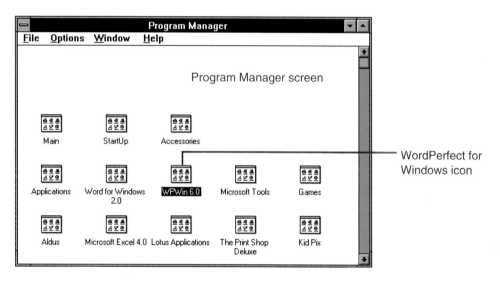

WordPerfect for Windows icon

TIP

If Your Screen Looks Different . . .

Depending on what programs are installed on your computer, your Program Manager screen might look slightly different from the screens in this book.

LEARNING THE LINGO

Documents: Work, such as a letter or a memo, created using a word processing program.

Icon: A small picture or graphic that represents a program, a command, or a piece of information.

Highlight: A solid color bar or outline around an icon or menu command that indicates you have selected it.

Starting WordPerfect for Windows

1 Locate the WordPerfect for Windows 6.0 icon in the Program Manager screen. Move your *mouse pointer* (arrow) directly on top of the icon, then double-click. If you prefer using the keyboard, press **Ctrl+Tab** until the icon is highlighted, then press **Enter**.

2 Move your mouse pointer until the arrow is positioned directly on top of the WordPerfect for Windows icon in the program group, and double-click. Or use the **arrow** keys on your keyboard until the icon is highlighted, then press **Enter**.

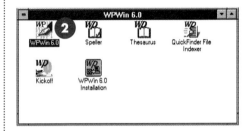

QUICK REFRESHER

As you learned in the Introduction, you can use the mouse to point and select items on-screen. Here are the mouse techniques you will need to use with the tasks in this section:

Point: To move your mouse so that the arrow on-screen is directly over the item you want to select.

Click: A quick, light tap of the left mouse button while holding the mouse pointer steadily over the item to be selected.

Double click: Two quick, light taps in a row on the left mouse button.

UNDERSTANDING THE WORDPERFECT SCREEN

What Are the Parts of the WordPerfect for Windows Screen?

When you start WordPerfect for Windows 6.0, your computer will display the screen shown in the figure below. You'll need to know about the parts of the screen in order to create your WordPerfect documents. It's a good idea to familiarize yourself with the screen before you begin the tasks in Part 2.

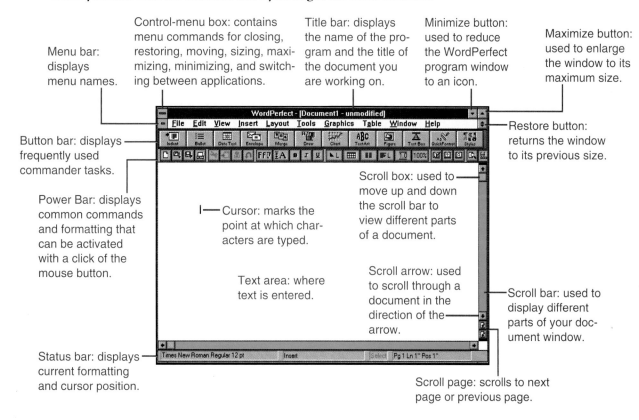

Control-menu box: contains menu commands for closing, restoring, moving, sizing, maximizing, minimizing, and switching between applications.

Title bar: displays the name of the program and the title of the document you are working on.

Minimize button: used to reduce the WordPerfect program window to an icon.

Maximize button: used to enlarge the window to its maximum size.

Menu bar: displays menu names.

Button bar: displays frequently used commander tasks.

Power Bar: displays common commands and formatting that can be activated with a click of the mouse button.

Restore button: returns the window to its previous size.

Scroll box: used to move up and down the scroll bar to view different parts of a document.

Cursor: marks the point at which characters are typed.

Text area: where text is entered.

Scroll arrow: used to scroll through a document in the direction of the arrow.

Scroll bar: used to display different parts of your document window.

Status bar: displays current formatting and cursor position.

Scroll page: scrolls to next page or previous page.

LEARNING THE LINGO

Commands: Orders that tell the computer what to do.

Formatting: Changes in the look of text, such as making it bolder and larger, or changing its position. Also called *attributes* or *text enhancements*.

USING WORDPERFECT MENUS

Why Use Menus?

Menus are used to give commands that tell WordPerfect what you want to do. Menus offer lists of commands to choose from. You'll find the menu names displayed on the menu bar on your screen. When you select a menu, it *pulls down* or opens up to reveal a list of commands like those shown in the figure below.

You can use the mouse or the keyboard to select menu commands. Notice that each menu name and command has an underlined letter. This is the *selection letter*. If you're using the keyboard to select a menu from the menu bar, you can hold down the **Alt** key and press the underlined selection letter to reveal the menu. When a menu list is revealed, you can choose commands from the list by typing the corresponding selection letter.

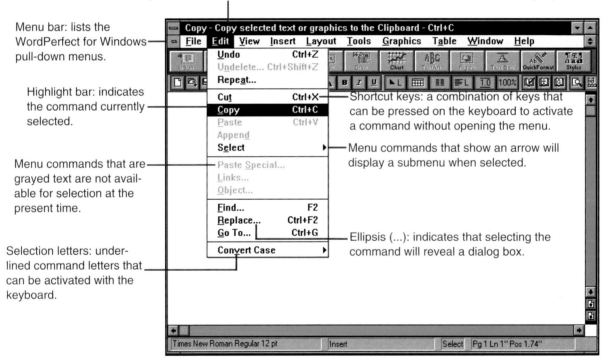

A description of what the command does will appear here when the command is highlighted.

Menu bar: lists the WordPerfect for Windows pull-down menus.

Highlight bar: indicates the command currently selected.

Menu commands that are grayed text are not available for selection at the present time.

Selection letters: underlined command letters that can be activated with the keyboard.

Shortcut keys: a combination of keys that can be pressed on the keyboard to activate a command without opening the menu.

Menu commands that show an arrow will display a submenu when selected.

Ellipsis (...): indicates that selecting the command will reveal a dialog box.

LEARNING THE LINGO

Selection letter: An underlined letter in the menu or command name. Keyboard users can type selection letters to activate commands or menus.

Shortcut key: A key, or combination of keys, that can be pressed to execute a command without opening menus.

Ellipsis: Three dots following a menu command which indicate a dialog box will appear when the command is selected.

Selecting Menu Commands

1 With the mouse, point at the menu name on the menu bar and click. If you're using the keyboard, press **Alt** to activate the menu bar, then type the underlined selection letter from the menu name.

2 To select a command from the menu displayed, click the mouse pointer to highlight the command (which also makes the selection). To use the keyboard, type the underlined selection letter.

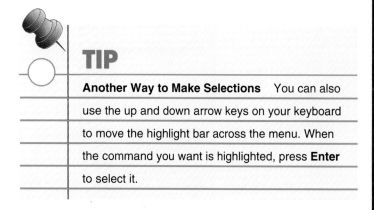

TIP

Changed Your Mind? If you display a menu or highlight a command, and then change your mind about using it, just press **Esc** twice, or click anywhere outside of the menu.

TIP

Another Way to Make Selections You can also use the up and down arrow keys on your keyboard to move the highlight bar across the menu. When the command you want is highlighted, press **Enter** to select it.

Basic WordPerfect for Windows Tasks

USING DIALOG BOXES

What Is a Dialog Box?

A *dialog box* is a separate window that appears when WordPerfect needs additional information to carry out a command. Menu commands that are followed by an *ellipsis* (...) will open a dialog box. Sometimes *command buttons* will open a dialog box too. Each dialog box is different, but they all share common elements.

You can use your mouse to click on the different parts of the dialog box, or you can use the keyboard by pressing the **Tab** key or choosing selection letters. Once all the settings in the dialog box are the way you want them, you can close the box to carry out the command or task.

Text box: information pertaining to the task you are performing is typed in this box.

List box: displays a list of items to choose from.

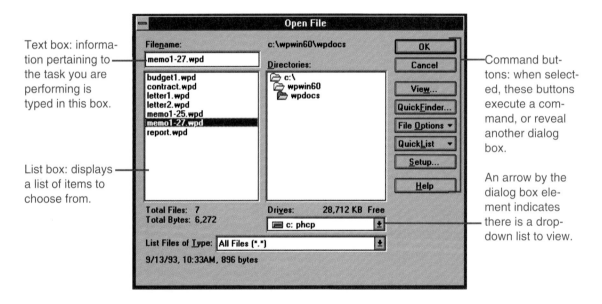

Command buttons: when selected, these buttons execute a command, or reveal another dialog box.

An arrow by the dialog box element indicates there is a drop-down list to view.

Option buttons: options that can be turned on or off with a dot. Only one option can be selected in a group of option buttons.

Check box: turns an attribute on or off with an x. Multiple check boxes can be selected.

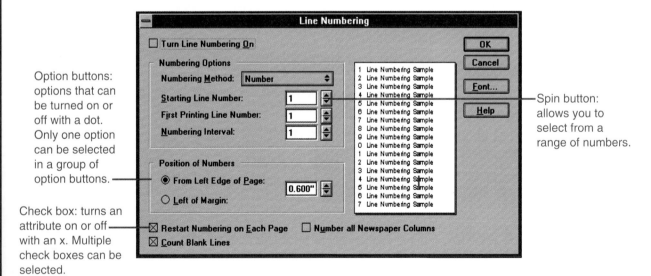

Spin button: allows you to select from a range of numbers.

How to Use a Dialog Box

To make selections in a dialog box, simply click on the items you want with the mouse, or press **Alt** and the underlined selection letter on the keyboard. You can also use the **Tab** key on the keyboard to move forward, and press **Shift+Tab** to move backward around the dialog box. (The highlighted area in a dialog box usually appears to have an outline around it, which means the area is active and ready for selections to be made.)

TIP

Dialog Box Mistakes?   To return to the document window without making any changes, use the **Cancel** button in the dialog box, or press **Esc**.

Dialog Box Elements

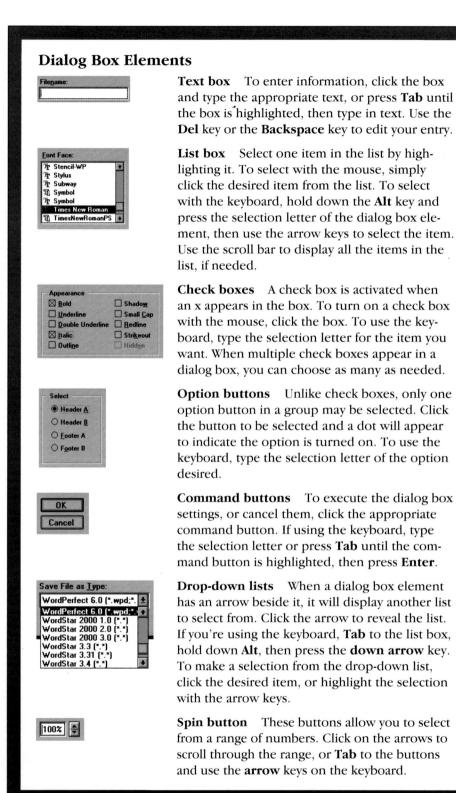

Text box   To enter information, click the box and type the appropriate text, or press **Tab** until the box is highlighted, then type in text. Use the **Del** key or the **Backspace** key to edit your entry.

List box   Select one item in the list by highlighting it. To select with the mouse, simply click the desired item from the list. To select with the keyboard, hold down the **Alt** key and press the selection letter of the dialog box element, then use the arrow keys to select the item. Use the scroll bar to display all the items in the list, if needed.

Check boxes   A check box is activated when an x appears in the box. To turn on a check box with the mouse, click the box. To use the keyboard, type the selection letter for the item you want. When multiple check boxes appear in a dialog box, you can choose as many as needed.

Option buttons   Unlike check boxes, only one option button in a group may be selected. Click the button to be selected and a dot will appear to indicate the option is turned on. To use the keyboard, type the selection letter of the option desired.

Command buttons   To execute the dialog box settings, or cancel them, click the appropriate command button. If using the keyboard, type the selection letter or press **Tab** until the command button is highlighted, then press **Enter**.

Drop-down lists   When a dialog box element has an arrow beside it, it will display another list to select from. Click the arrow to reveal the list. If you're using the keyboard, **Tab** to the list box, hold down **Alt**, then press the **down arrow** key. To make a selection from the drop-down list, click the desired item, or highlight the selection with the arrow keys.

Spin button   These buttons allow you to select from a range of numbers. Click on the arrows to scroll through the range, or **Tab** to the buttons and use the **arrow** keys on the keyboard.

USING THE POWER BAR

What Is a Power Bar?

At the top of your WordPerfect for Windows 6.0 screen, below the Button Bar, is a row of buttons with various icons. This is called the *Power Bar*. On the Power Bar you'll find buttons representing many of the common WordPerfect commands and formatting controls. These buttons are shortcuts to commands found on the menu lists. Selecting a button from the Power Bar can be a lot faster than pulling down menu lists and choosing commands.

To select the Power Bar buttons, use the mouse pointer to point and click (or to press and hold) on the desired button. Some buttons will execute a command right away (such as **Paste**). Other buttons (such as the **Font** button) will display a menu list. Still other buttons will open a dialog box (such as the **Print** button). Sorry, you can't use the keyboard to select the buttons.

To find out what kind of command or task the button represents, point to the button (but don't click), and look at the Title bar. A brief description of the command appears, along with any shortcut keys for keyboard users.

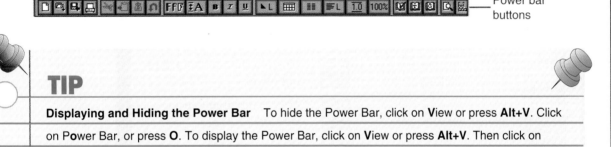

Power bar buttons

TIP

Displaying and Hiding the Power Bar   To hide the Power Bar, click on **V**iew or press **Alt+V**. Click on **P**ower Bar, or press **O**. To display the Power Bar, click on **V**iew or press **Alt+V**. Then click on **P**ower Bar, or press **O**.

Power Bar Tools

 Starts a new document.

 Opens an existing document.

 Saves the current document.

 Prints the current document.

 Cuts selected text or graphics to the Clipboard.

 Copies selected text or graphics to the Clipboard.

 Pastes text or graphics from the Clipboard into your document.

 Undoes the last edit made.

 Changes the font.

 Changes the font size.

 Changes text to bold.

 Changes text to italics.

 Changes text to underline.

 Specifies tab stops and positions.

 Creates a table.

 Creates columns.

 Aligns text left, right, or center.

 Specifies line spacing of text.

 Magnifies text to get a closer look at details.

 Checks the spelling in your document.

 Opens a thesaurus for finding words.

 Checks the grammar in your document.

 Displays an entire document page

 Displays or hides the Button Bar.

USING THE BUTTON BAR

What Is a Button Bar?

The *Button Bar* is a bar at the top of your screen below the menu bar that allows you to automate frequently-used commands or tasks that aren't already handled by the Power Bar. (See the "Using the Power Bar" task.) For example, if your document requires several insertions of the current date, it would be much easier to have a button to automatically do this when needed rather than typing in the date each time. That's where the Button Bar comes in handy. A quick click on a button inserts the current date into your document automatically.

When you start WordPerfect for Windows the first time, the Button Bar is automatically displayed. To activate a command or task, simply click on the desired button. To find out what kind of command or task the button represents, point to the button and look at the Title bar. A brief description of the command appears, along with any shortcut keys for keyboard users.

 ────Button bar

TIP

Unknown Commands   Some of the icons on the Button Bar represent commands or tasks that are not covered in this book. Refer to the Help system or program documentation for more information.

TIP

Moving the Button Bar   You can reposition the Button Bar to appear in other locations on your screen. Place your mouse pointer in a blank area of the Button Bar so that the pointer becomes a hand icon. Hold down the mouse button, and drag the Button Bar to a new location on the screen.

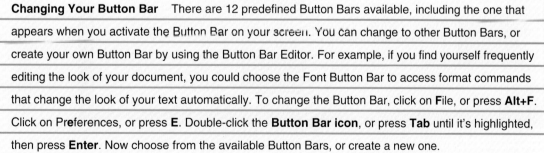

TIP

Changing Your Button Bar   There are 12 predefined Button Bars available, including the one that appears when you activate the Button Bar on your screen. You can change to other Button Bars, or create your own Button Bar by using the Button Bar Editor. For example, if you find yourself frequently editing the look of your document, you could choose the Font Button Bar to access format commands that change the look of your text automatically. To change the Button Bar, click on File, or press **Alt+F**. Click on Preferences, or press **E**. Double-click the **Button Bar icon**, or press **Tab** until it's highlighted, then press **Enter**. Now choose from the available Button Bars, or create a new one.

USING THE BUTTON BAR

Turning the Button Bar On or Off

1 Click on **View**, or press **Alt+V**.

2 Click on Button **B**ar, or press **B**. A checkmark next to the command indicates the Button Bar will be revealed. If there is no checkmark, the Button Bar will be hidden

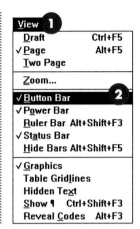

Button Bar Tools

 Indents a paragraph by one tab stop.

 Inserts bullets or numbers into your document.

 Inserts the current date into your document.

 Creates an envelope.

 Combines data files and form files.

 Starts WordPerfect for Windows drawing program.

 Makes charts with the drawing program.

 The TextArt button allows you to create special effects for your text.

 Retrieves a graphic.

 Creates a text block.

 Applies formatting from one selected block to another selected block.

 Creates, edits, and applies formatting styles.

GETTING HELP

What Is Help?

Help is exactly what it sounds like—on-screen assistance from the WordPerfect program for any problems you encounter. For example, if you were in the midst of saving a document and an unfamiliar dialog box appeared on your screen, you could access the online Help feature to find out what to do.

There are several Help options to choose from the **Help** menu, including a glossary and specific information about using Help. The WordPerfect Help system is also *context-sensitive*, meaning that you can get help when you're in the middle of a task. Help knows what point in the program you are seeking help for. It will take you directly to the Help section that explains all about the task you are trying to perform.

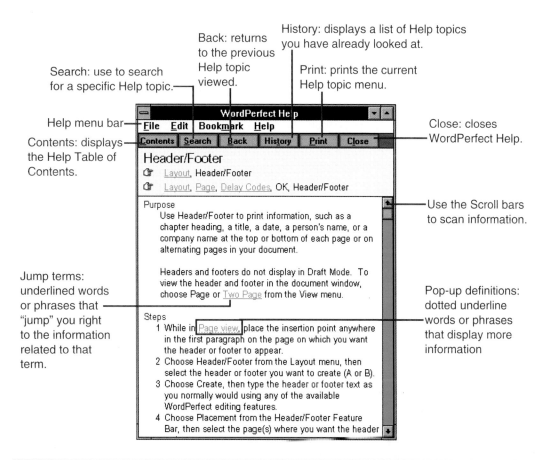

Search: use to search for a specific Help topic.

Back: returns to the previous Help topic viewed.

History: displays a list of Help topics you have already looked at.

Print: prints the current Help topic menu.

Help menu bar

Contents: displays the Help Table of Contents.

Close: closes WordPerfect Help.

Use the Scroll bars to scan information.

Jump terms: underlined words or phrases that "jump" you right to the information related to that term.

Pop-up definitions: dotted underline words or phrases that display more information

WordPerfect Help

File   Edit   Bookmark   Help

Contents | Search | Back | History | Print | Close

Header/Footer
☞ Layout, Header/Footer
☞ Layout, Page, Delay Codes, OK, Header/Footer

Purpose
Use Header/Footer to print information, such as a chapter heading, a title, a date, a person's name, or a company name at the top or bottom of each page or on alternating pages in your document.

Headers and footers do not display in Draft Mode. To view the header and footer in the document window, choose Page or Two Page from the View menu.

Steps
1 While in Page view, place the insertion point anywhere in the first paragraph on the page on which you want the header or footer to appear.
2 Choose Header/Footer from the Layout menu, then select the header or footer you want to create (A or B).
3 Choose Create, then type the header or footer text as you normally would using any of the available WordPerfect editing features.
4 Choose Placement from the Header/Footer Feature Bar, then select the page(s) where you want the header

---

LEARNING THE LINGO

Context-sensitive: A help system that takes you directly to the information pertaining to the task you are trying to perform, without routing you through a topical index.

Basic WordPerfect for Windows Tasks

GETTING HELP

Getting Help

1 Click on **Help**, or press **Alt+H**.

2 Click on Contents, or press **C**.

3 When the Help contents window opens, click on the underlined topic you want to view, or press tab to highlight the words, then press Enter. Click on the Help command buttons at the top to assist your search. Keyboard users should press selection letters to activate command buttons.

TIP

Help in a Jiffy   If you're in the middle of a document, you can get help right away by pressing **F1**. Or you can use the *What Is* feature by pressing **Shift+F1**. The What Is feature turns your mouse pointer into a question-mark icon with a thought bubble. Using this pointer, point to the part of the screen on which you want information, and click.

Exercise

Follow these steps to practice using the Help feature.

1 Click on **Help**, or press **Alt+H**.

2 Click on **Contents**, or press **C**.

3 Click on **How Do I** under the Choose list of jump terms, or press **Tab** until the words are highlighted, and then press **Enter**.

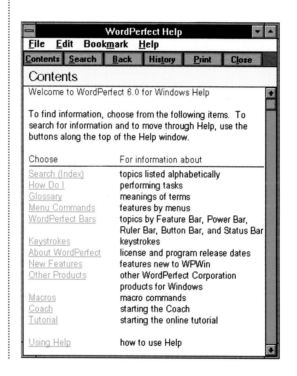

TIP

Quick Exit   To exit from the Help system quickly, press **Alt+F4**.

Basic WordPerfect for Windows Tasks

4 Click on the underlined topic you want to view, or press **Tab** until the topic is highlighted, and then press **Enter**.

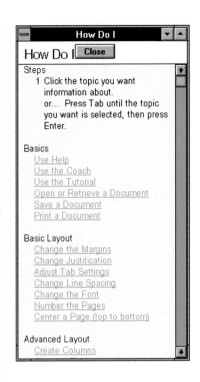

5 Click on the scroll bar arrows to display different sections of the topic, or use the **arrow** keys, **PgUp** and **PgDn** keys to view the section with the keyboard.

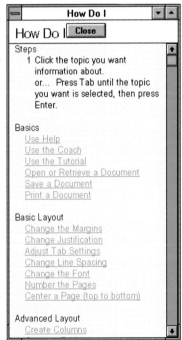

6 To exit, click on **F**ile, then click on E**x**it. To exit with the keyboard, press **Alt+F**, then type **X**.

EXITING WORDPERFECT FOR WINDOWS

When Do I Exit WordPerfect?

When you've finished working with WordPerfect for Windows, you should always *exit* the program, providing you have saved your documents.

Exiting WordPerfect for Windows

1 Click on File, or press **Alt+F**.

2 Click on Exit, or press **X**.

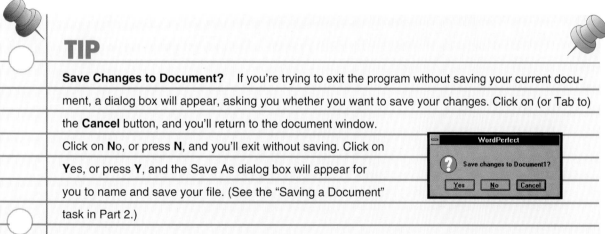

TIP

Save Changes to Document?   If you're trying to exit the program without saving your current document, a dialog box will appear, asking you whether you want to save your changes. Click on (or Tab to) the **Cancel** button, and you'll return to the document window.

Click on **No**, or press **N**, and you'll exit without saving. Click on Yes, or press **Y**, and the Save As dialog box will appear for you to name and save your file. (See the "Saving a Document" task in Part 2.)

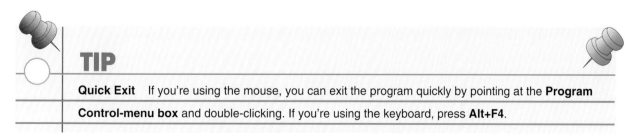

TIP

Quick Exit   If you're using the mouse, you can exit the program quickly by pointing at the **Program Control-menu box** and double-clicking. If you're using the keyboard, press **Alt+F4**.

PART 2

Creating, Editing, Saving, and Printing Documents

In this section, you'll learn how to work with your WordPerfect documents. You'll develop the basic skills needed to enter text, edit your text, save your work, and print it all out.

You'll learn about:

- Entering Text
- Moving Around the Document Window
- Insert and Typeover Modes
- Correcting Mistakes
- Selecting Text
- Deleting Text
- Moving Text

- Copying Text
- Saving a Document
- Opening a Document
- Finding and Replacing Text
- Zooming In and Out
- Working with Multiple Documents
- Printing a Document

ENTERING TEXT

How Do You Type In Text?

When you start WordPerfect for Windows, your screen displays a new document, ready and waiting for action. Entering text is quite simple—just start typing. The open area on your screen is where your text appears. The blinking line where characters enter the screen is called the *cursor*, or *insertion point*. When you start WordPerfect for Windows, the cursor is at the top of the page ready to go. (Your document has a 1-inch default margin on all four sides. To learn about adjusting margins, read the "Setting Margins" task in Part 3.)

You can move the insertion point by moving the mouse pointer to a new position and clicking the cursor into place, or by using the arrow keys on the keyboard. As you type, the cursor moves to the right, advancing automatically to the next line when you've run out of room. This means you don't have to press the Enter key to signify a new line. WordPerfect "wraps" your sentence to the next line automatically. The only time you need to press the Enter key is when you're ready to begin a new paragraph.

WordPerfect documents are broken down into paragraphs. A paragraph can be a single line, a grouping of text, or even bulleted copy.

A regular text block paragraph.

A heading is also a paragraph.

This bulleted list is a paragraph too.

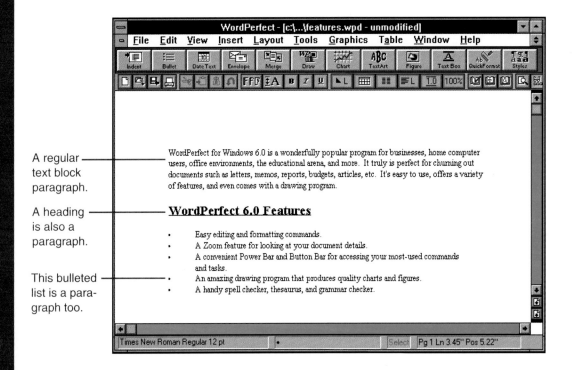

Typing Text

1 Starting at the cursor positioned at the top of your document, type your text.

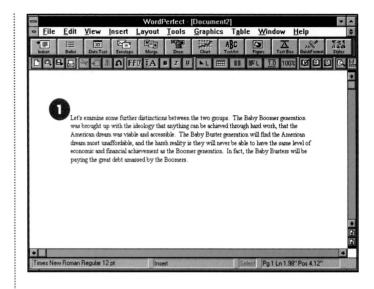

2 At the end of a paragraph, press **Enter**.

LEARNING THE LINGO

Cursor: A blinking vertical line that indicates where typed characters will appear. Also known as the *insertion point*.

Wrapping: When your text reaches the end of a line, the cursor moves to the start of the next line automatically.

Paragraph: A group of words that are treated as a block of text. Paragraphs can also be single lines, captions, bulleted text, and even blank lines. A paragraph is created by pressing the **Enter** key at the end of a line.

Bulleted copy: A text list with *bullet* symbols, or small dots, in front of each listed item. Bulleted lists are used to emphasize text in your document.

TIP

Hard and Soft Returns   When you press **Enter** at the end of a line, it's considered a *hard return*.

This allows you to begin a new line of text in a new paragraph. When you let WordPerfect wrap text at

the end of the line, it's called a *soft return*.

Creating, Editing, Saving, and Printing Documents

ENTERING TEXT

Exercise

To practice entering text and moving the cursor across the screen, type in the text shown following the steps below.

1 Type the date and press **Enter** four times.

2 Type **Dear Mr. Willard:** and press **Enter** twice.

3 Type the two sentences of the letter, then press **Enter** four times.

4 Type **Sincerely,** and press **Enter** four times.

5 Type your name.

6 Position the cursor immediately after the word "Friday" in the first sentence, then type a comma.

7 Position the cursor immediately after the last sentence, then type **We look forward to your attendance.**

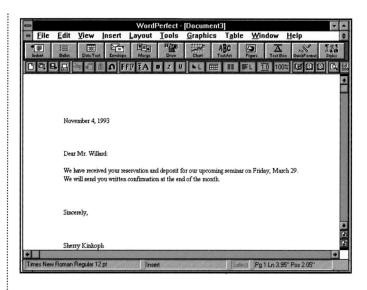

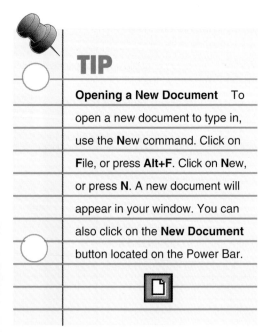

TIP

Opening a New Document   To open a new document to type in, use the **N**ew command. Click on **F**ile, or press **Alt+F**. Click on **N**ew, or press **N**. A new document will appear in your window. You can also click on the **New Document** button located on the Power Bar.

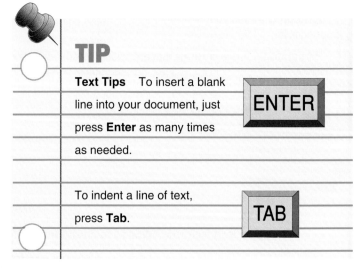

TIP

Text Tips   To insert a blank line into your document, just press **Enter** as many times as needed.

To indent a line of text, press **Tab**.

TIP

Need a New Page? To insert a page break in your document, follow these steps:

1. Click the cursor where
   you want the page
   break to occur.

2. Click on **I**nsert, or
   press **Alt+I**.

3. Click on **P**age Break,
   or press **P**.

A solid ruled line will appear in
your document, indicating where
the page break occurs.

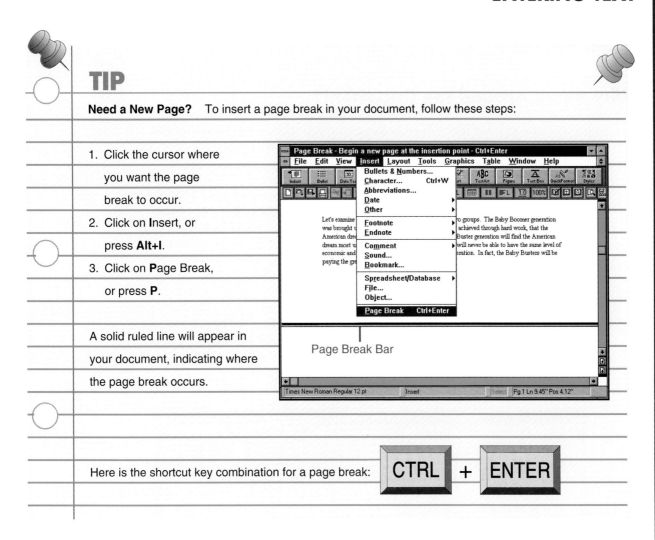

Page Break Bar

Here is the shortcut key combination for a page break: CTRL + ENTER

Creating, Editing, Saving, and Printing Documents

MOVING AROUND THE DOCUMENT WINDOW

Why Move Around the Document?

Once you have entered text into your document, you'll invariably have occasion to make changes. To change (or *edit*) your text, you'll need to know how to move around in the document window.

When moving the mouse pointer around the document window, you'll notice it changes appearance, depending on where it's located on the screen. When the mouse pointer is located in the text area of your document, it will look like a capital "I." This is called an *I-beam*. When the mouse pointer is moved anywhere outside the text area, it becomes a small arrow. At the left side of the text area is an invisible *selection bar*, just to the left of the margin. When placed here, the mouse pointer becomes an arrow pointing "northeast."

When inside the text area, you can place the cursor by moving the mouse pointer to a new position and clicking the cursor into place. To make selections outside the text area, move the mouse pointer and click on the elements you want to select.

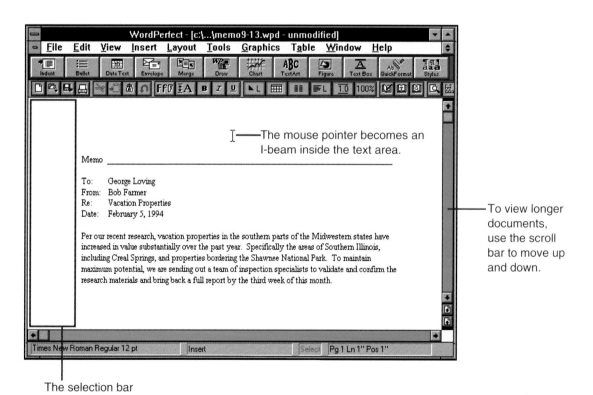

The mouse pointer becomes an I-beam inside the text area.

To view longer documents, use the scroll bar to move up and down.

The selection bar

Moving Around with the Keyboard

You can move around the document window with the keyboard by pressing the *cursor movement keys*, such as the arrow keys, or *combination keys*, such as **Ctrl+Home**.

Press	To move the cursor
↑	Up one line
↓	Down one line
→	Right one character
←	Left one character
HOME	Beginning of the current line
END	End of the current line
CTRL + HOME	Beginning of the document
CTRL + END	End of the document
CTRL + ↑	Beginning of the current or previous paragraph
CTRL + ↓	Beginning of next paragraph
CTRL + →	Beginning of the next word
CTRL + ←	Beginning of the current word or previous word

LEARNING THE LINGO

Edit: To make changes in your text, or otherwise modify your document.

I-beam: The mouse pointer's capital-I shape when it is anywhere inside the text area of your screen.

Selection bar: The narrow area to the left of the left margin, used to select blocks of text. Placing the mouse pointer here turns it to an arrow.

Creating, Editing, Saving, and Printing Documents

INSERT AND TYPEOVER MODES

When to Use Insert and Typeover

There are two *modes* (or ways of operating) for entering text in WordPerfect for Windows. In *Insert mode*, existing text moves to the right to make room for new text typed in at the cursor. With *typeover* (or overstrike) mode, existing text is replaced with new text typed in. In Typeover mode, you type over any existing text.

TIP

Insert by Default   When you start WordPerfect for Windows 6.0, it's always in Insert mode unless you change it to Typeover mode.

LEARNING THE LINGO

Insert mode: Adding text between existing text without deleting any existing characters. Existing text is shifted to the right as new text is typed.

Typeover mode: Adding text that takes the place of (types over) existing text. Also called *overstrike mode*.

Entering Text in Insert and Typeover Modes

1 Position the cursor where you want new text to appear by clicking the cursor into place with the mouse, or using the **arrow** keys.

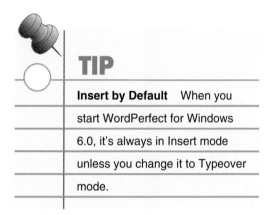

2 Press the **Insert** key on the keyboard to switch back and forth between Insert and Typeover modes.

Exercise

To practice using the Insert and Typeover modes, type in the text shown, and follow these steps.

1 Change to Typeover mode by pressing **Insert**, move the cursor to the left of the number 4 at the end of the date, then type a **3**.

2 Press **Insert** to change the mode back to Insert mode, and move the cursor to the beginning of the word "contribution" in the first sentence. Type **generous** and a space.

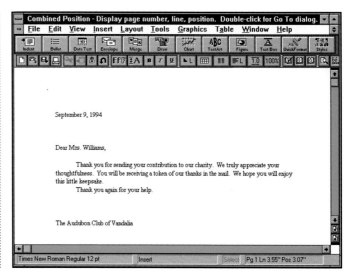

September 9, 1994

Dear Mrs. Williams,

Thank you for sending your contribution to our charity. We truly appreciate your thoughtfulness. You will be receiving a token of our thanks in the mail. We hope you will enjoy this little keepsake.
Thank you again for your help.

The Audubon Club of Vandalia

Creating, Editing, Saving, and Printing Documents

CORRECTING MISTAKES

How Do You Correct Text?

A time-saving feature of any word processing program is the capability of correcting mistakes. With WordPerfect for Windows, you can fix errors easily using the mouse or keyboard. To fix minor mistakes, use the **Delete** or **Backspace** keys.

Correcting Text

1 Move the cursor to the text you want to delete.

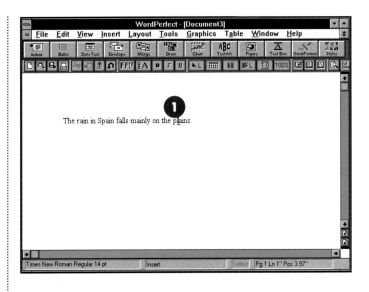

2 Press **Delete** to erase a character to the right of the cursor, or **Backspace** to erase a character to the left of the cursor.

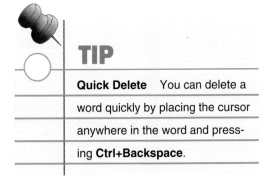

TIP

Quick Delete   You can delete a word quickly by placing the cursor anywhere in the word and pressing **Ctrl+Backspace**.

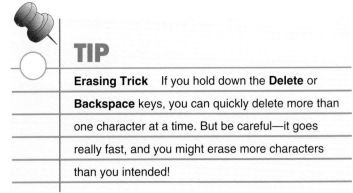

TIP

Erasing Trick   If you hold down the **Delete** or **Backspace** keys, you can quickly delete more than one character at a time. But be careful—it goes really fast, and you might erase more characters than you intended!

Exercise

Type in the sentence shown, and follow these steps to practice using the Delete and Backspace keys.

① Position the cursor at the end of the word "Spain."

② Press **Backspace** until the words "in Spain." are deleted.

③ Position the cursor at the beginning of the word "mainly."

④ Press **Delete** until the word is erased.

Creating, Editing, Saving, and Printing Documents

SELECTING TEXT

Why Select Text?

To edit (that is, change) larger portions of your text, you must learn to select the text portion you wish to modify. Anytime you want to move or copy text, or assign formatting, you must first *select* (or *highlight*) the text portion to be changed.

Selected text has a solid block of black surrounding the word or words. Instead of black characters on a white background, highlighted text shows white characters on a black background. (Also called reverse text.)

You can select a character, a word, a sentence, a paragraph, or an entire document. The selected text is called a *text block*. Once a text block has been selected, various command functions can be applied to the highlighted text.

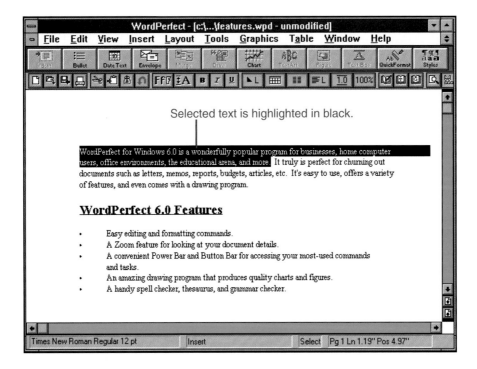

Selected text is highlighted in black.

LEARNING THE LINGO

Highlight: A black background or bar that surrounds a word or group of words that indicate the text is selected and commands can be executed that will affect that text.

Text Block: Any amount of text, ranging from a single character to an entire document, that you want to work with.

Formatting: Changing the look of text, such as making it bolder, larger, or positioning.

Selecting Text with the Mouse

1 Point to the first letter of the text block you want to select.

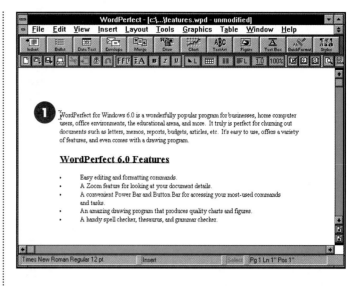

2 Press and hold down the left mouse button and drag the mouse pointer to the last character of text you want highlighted.

3 Release the mouse button and the text block has been selected.

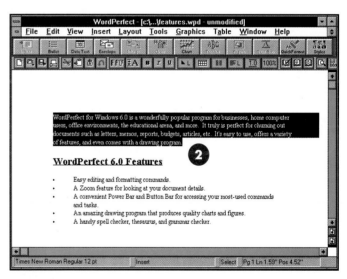

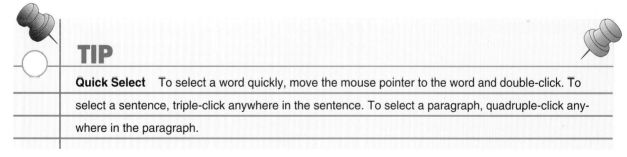

TIP

Quick Select To select a word quickly, move the mouse pointer to the word and double-click. To select a sentence, triple-click anywhere in the sentence. To select a paragraph, quadruple-click anywhere in the paragraph.

Creating, Editing, Saving, and Printing Documents

SELECTING TEXT

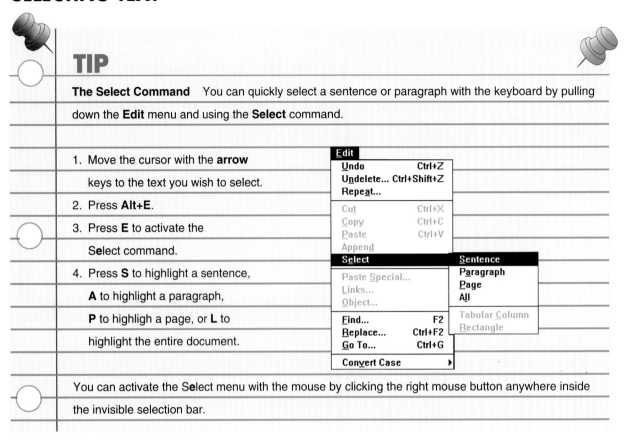

TIP

The Select Command   You can quickly select a sentence or paragraph with the keyboard by pulling down the **Edit** menu and using the **Select** command.

1. Move the cursor with the **arrow** keys to the text you wish to select.

2. Press **Alt+E**.

3. Press **E** to activate the Select command.

4. Press **S** to highlight a sentence, **A** to highlight a paragraph, **P** to highligh a page, or **L** to highlight the entire document.

Edit	
U**n**do	Ctrl+Z
U**n**delete...	Ctrl+Shift+Z
Repe**a**t...	
Cu**t**	Ctrl+X
Copy	Ctrl+C
Paste	Ctrl+V
Appen**d**	
Select	▸
Paste **S**pecial...	
Lin**k**s...	
Object...	
Find...	F2
Replace...	Ctrl+F2
Go To...	Ctrl+G
Con**v**ert Case	▸

Select submenu: Sentence, Paragraph, Page, All, Tabular Column, Rectangle

You can activate the Select menu with the mouse by clicking the right mouse button anywhere inside the invisible selection bar.

Selecting Text with the Keyboard

1 With the **arrow** keys, point to the first letter of the text block you want to select.

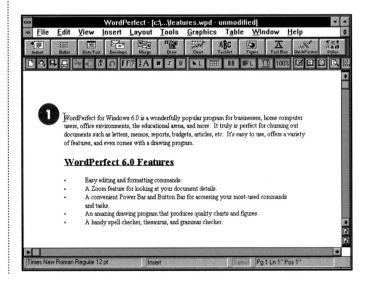

2 Press **F8**.

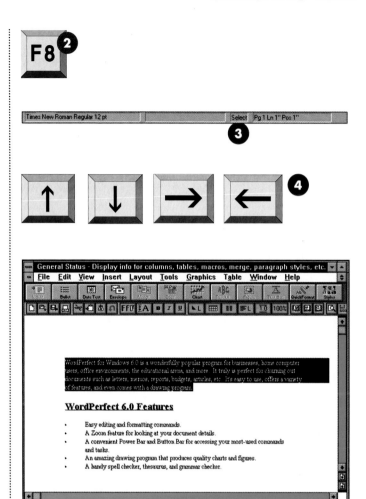

3 Check the status bar to make sure the "Select" mode is on.

4 Press the **arrow** keys, or any of the cursor movement keys and key combinations, to highlight text. Stop highlighting when the last letter of the text block has been selected.

TIP

The Invisible Selection Bar You can use an invisible selection bar at the left side of your left margin to select blocks of text. When moved to this area, the mouse pointer becomes an arrow that points "northeast." Use clicking or clicking and dragging motions to quickly highlight blocks of text.

SELECTING TEXT

If you're using the keyboard to select text, you can press **F8** and the following cursor movement keys.

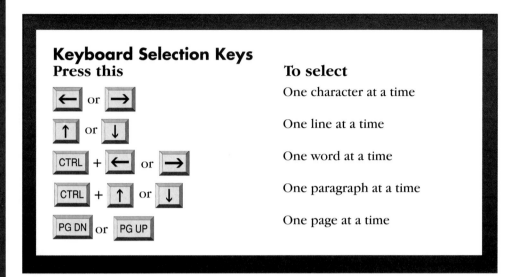

Keyboard Selection Keys

Press this	To select
← or →	One character at a time
↑ or ↓	One line at a time
CTRL + ← or →	One word at a time
CTRL + ↑ or ↓	One paragraph at a time
PG DN or PG UP	One page at a time

TIP

Select the Wrong Text?

If you've accidentally highlighted some text you don't want to select, click anywhere in the document, or press **F8** to cancel the selection.

TIP

Fast Keyboard Selection   You can also hold down the **Shift** key and press the **arrow** keys to select characters in your document. For example, to select one character, place the cursor next to the character, hold down the **Shift** key, and press the → key. This method highlights one character at a time.

To select more than one character, hold down the **Shift** key and the **Ctrl** key, then press the **arrow** keys.

When Can Text Be Deleted?

In the task "Correcting Mistakes," you learned how to delete small amounts of text using the **Delete** and **Backspace** keys. Pecking away at the **Delete** or **Backspace** keys is a slow process when you need to erase larger amounts of text. An easier method is to delete *blocks* of text.

Before you can delete a block of text, you must first select or highlight it. To learn how to select text, turn to the "Selecting Text Blocks" task found earlier in this section.

Deleting Text

1 Select the text to be deleted.

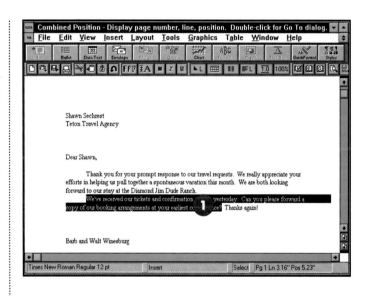

2 Press **Delete**.

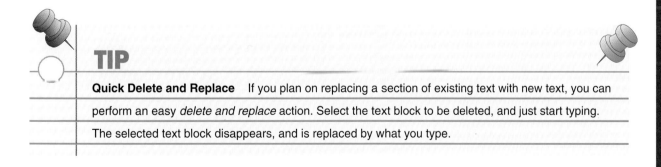

TIP

Quick Delete and Replace   If you plan on replacing a section of existing text with new text, you can perform an easy *delete and replace* action. Select the text block to be deleted, and just start typing. The selected text block disappears, and is replaced by what you type.

DELETING TEXT

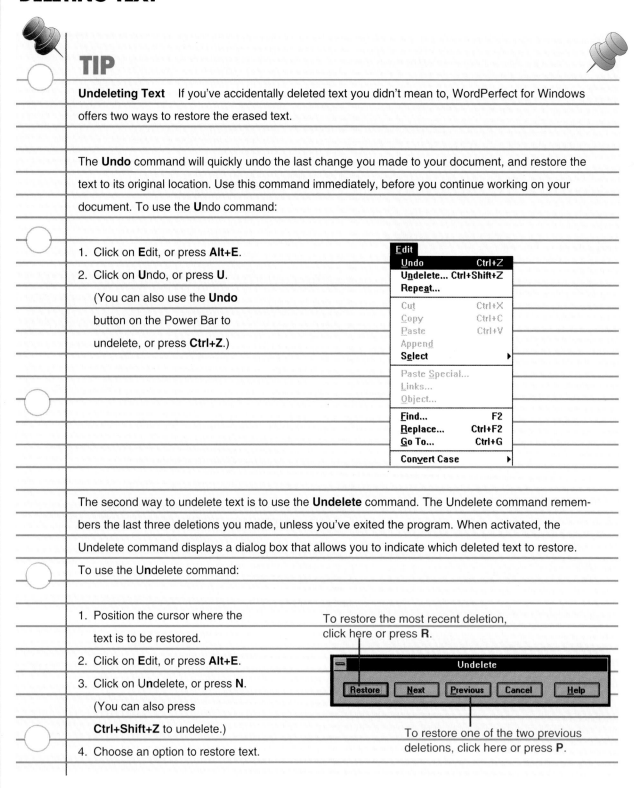

TIP

Undeleting Text   If you've accidentally deleted text you didn't mean to, WordPerfect for Windows offers two ways to restore the erased text.

The **Undo** command will quickly undo the last change you made to your document, and restore the text to its original location. Use this command immediately, before you continue working on your document. To use the **U**ndo command:

1. Click on **E**dit, or press **Alt+E**.

2. Click on **U**ndo, or press **U**.

   (You can also use the **Undo** button on the Power Bar to undelete, or press **Ctrl+Z**.)

The second way to undelete text is to use the **Undelete** command. The Undelete command remembers the last three deletions you made, unless you've exited the program. When activated, the Undelete command displays a dialog box that allows you to indicate which deleted text to restore. To use the **Un**delete command:

1. Position the cursor where the text is to be restored.

   To restore the most recent deletion, click here or press **R**.

2. Click on **E**dit, or press **Alt+E**.

3. Click on **Un**delete, or press **N**.

   (You can also press **Ctrl+Shift+Z** to undelete.)

4. Choose an option to restore text.

   To restore one of the two previous deletions, click here or press **P**.

48

Exercise

Type in the text shown, and practice deleting a block of text following these steps:

1 Position the cursor at the beginning of the second paragraph.

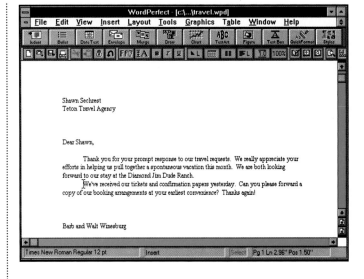

2 Press and drag the mouse until the entire paragraph is selected, then release the mouse button. If using the keyboard, use the **arrow** keys to highlight the block.

3 Press **Delete**.

MOVING TEXT

Why Move Text?

A marvelous feature of word processing programs is the ability to move text around in a document without retyping. For example, you might want to move a paragraph from the middle to the beginning of your document, or from one document into another.

When text is moved, it's held in a temporary storage area called the *Clipboard*. When you're ready to place the text in another part of your document, it's moved from the Clipboard to your current cursor position. You can use the Clipboard to move text to other documents, or to other Windows programs.

LEARNING THE LINGO

Clipboard: A temporary storage area for text and graphics.

TIP

Cut and Paste Shortcuts   If you're using the keyboard to enter commands, here are some shortcut keys to cutting and pasting. Rather than activating the **E**dit menu to cut, press **Shift+Delete**; press **Shift+Insert** to paste.

Moving Text

 Select the text you want to move.

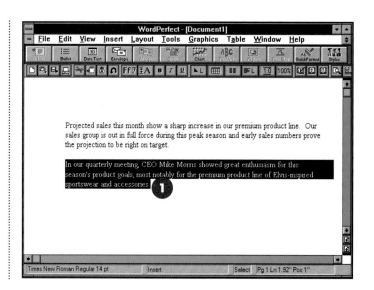

2 Click on **Edit**, or press **Alt+E**.

3 Click on **Cut**, or press **T**.

4 Position the cursor at the location to which you want to move the text.

Projected sales this month show a sharp increase in our premium product line. Our sales group is out in full force during this peak season and early sales numbers prove the projection to be right on target.

5 Click on **Edit**, or press **Alt+E**.

6 Click on **Paste**, or press **P**.

51

MOVING TEXT

Exercise

Type in the text shown, and practice moving a block of text following these steps:

1 Position the cursor at the beginning of the second paragraph.

2 Select the entire paragraph. To select with the mouse, press and hold the left mouse button, drag the mouse until the entire paragraph is highlighted, then release the mouse button. If using the keyboard, use the **arrow** keys to highlight the block.

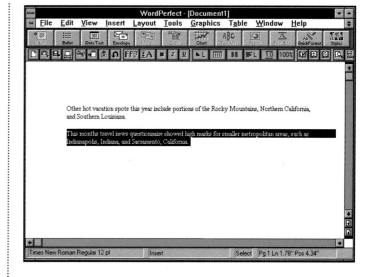

3 Click on **E**dit, or press **Alt+E**.

4 Click on Cu**t**, or press **T**.

5 Position the cursor at the beginning of the document.

6 Click on **E**dit, or press **Alt+E**.

7 Click on **P**aste, or press **P**.

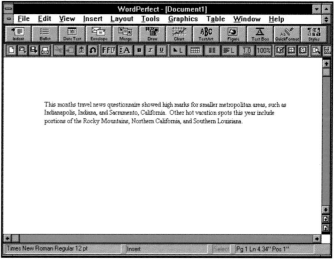

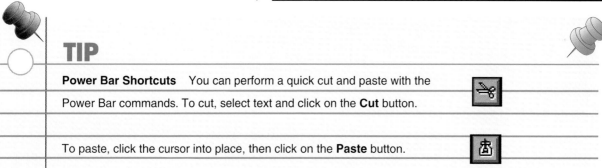

TIP

Power Bar Shortcuts   You can perform a quick cut and paste with the
Power Bar commands. To cut, select text and click on the **Cut** button.

To paste, click the cursor into place, then click on the **Paste** button.

COPYING TEXT

Why Copy Text?

There are times you'll want to copy text into another area in your document, into a different document, or into another Windows program. With the Windows Clipboard, copying is a simple procedure.

When text is copied, the copy is held in a temporary storage area called the *Clipboard*. When you're ready to place the copy in another part of your document, it's moved from the Clipboard to your current cursor position.

Copying Text

1 Select the text that you want to copy.

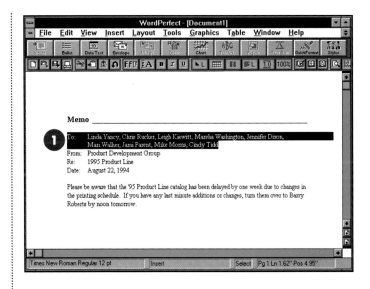

2 Click on **Edit**, or press **Alt+E**.

3 Click on **Copy**, or press **C**.

53

COPYING TEXT

4 Position the cursor at the location to which you want to copy the text.

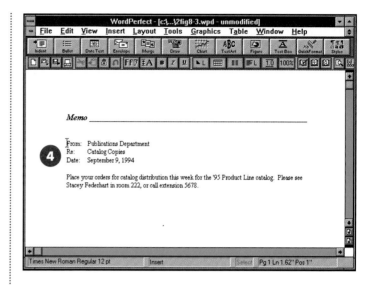

5 Click on **Edit**, or press **Alt+E**.

6 Click on **Paste**, or press **P**.

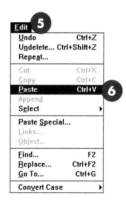

TIP

Copy and Paste Shortcuts   If you're using the keyboard to enter commands, here are some shortcut keys to copying and pasting. Rather than activating the Edit menu to copy, press **Ctrl+Insert**; press **Shift+Insert** to paste.

TIP

Power Bar Shortcuts   You can perform a quick copy and paste with the Power Bar commands.

To copy, select text and click on the **Copy** button.

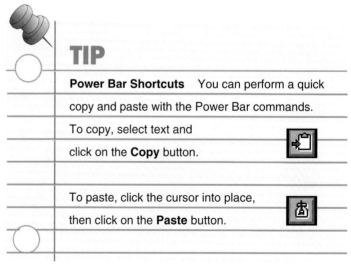

To paste, click the cursor into place, then click on the **Paste** button.

54

Exercise

Type in the text shown and practice copying a block of text following these steps:

1 Position the cursor at the beginning of the paragraph.

2 Select the entire paragraph. To select with the mouse, press and hold the left mouse button, drag the mouse until the entire paragraph is highlighted, then release the mouse button. If using the keyboard, use the **arrow** keys to highlight the block.

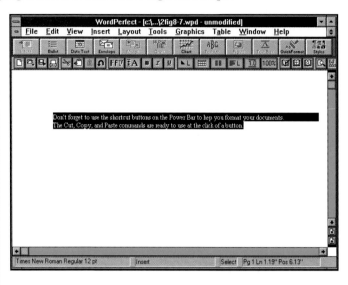

3 Click on **Edit**, or press **Alt+E**.

4 Click on **Copy**, or press **C**.

5 Position the cursor at the end of the paragraph.

6 Click on **Edit**, or press **Alt+E**.

7 Click on **Paste**, or press **P**.

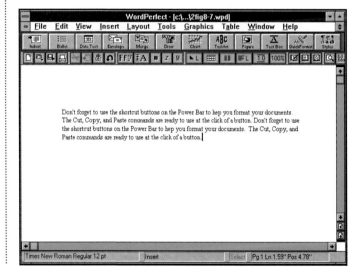

Creating, Editing, Saving, and Printing Documents

SAVING A DOCUMENT

When Is Saving Necessary?

Whenever you're ready to quit the program, and want to keep all your work intact, it's time to save your document. When you save a document, you can store it on your computer's hard disk or on a floppy disk. At the point of saving your document, or file, you must give it a name.

In WordPerfect for Windows, the *file name* can be up to eight characters long. File names can be descriptive, such as MEMO1, or REPORT. You can also add a *file extension* to your document name. SMITH.LTR, for example, has a .LTR extension indicating the document is a letter. File extensions can help you organize your files by type. This is helpful when looking for files later. Extensions begin with a period, and are up to three characters long.

The filename is typed here.

Select a different directory to save a document in by choosing from the Directories List box.

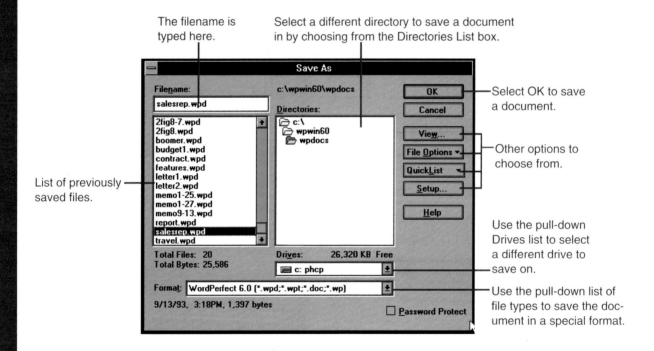

List of previously saved files.

Select OK to save a document.

Other options to choose from.

Use the pull-down Drives list to select a different drive to save on.

Use the pull-down list of file types to save the document in a special format.

LEARNING THE LINGO

File: Whenever you save a document, the information is saved in a file. Files are given unique names that distinguish them from other files.

File extension: An extra name added to the file name that helps determine what kind of file it is, such as .LTR (SMITH.LTR) or .DOC (REPORT.DOC).

Saving and Naming a Document

1 Click on the **File** menu, or press **Alt+F**.

2 Click on **Save**, or press **S**.

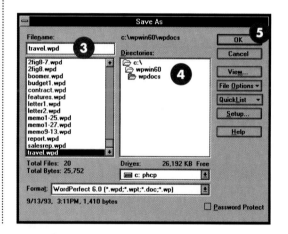

3 Type in a file name for the document.

4 Change the Directory, drive, or file type if necessary.

5 Click on **OK**, or press **Enter**.

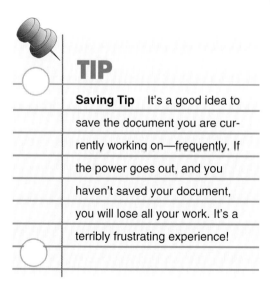

TIP

Saving Tip It's a good idea to save the document you are currently working on—frequently. If the power goes out, and you haven't saved your document, you will lose all your work. It's a terribly frustrating experience!

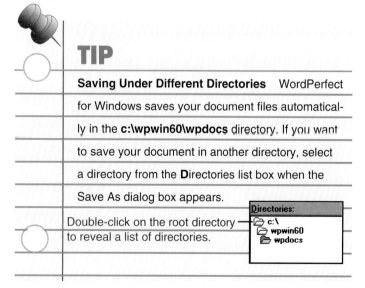

TIP

Saving Under Different Directories WordPerfect for Windows saves your document files automatically in the **c:\wpwin60\wpdocs** directory. If you want to save your document in another directory, select a directory from the **D**irectories list box when the Save As dialog box appears.

Double-click on the root directory to reveal a list of directories.

SAVING A DOCUMENT

TIP

The Save As Command   Sometimes you may wish to make slight changes to a document (such as a salutation or date), and give the changed document a new name, but keep the original intact. The Save **A**s command is a handy feature that allows you to do just that. For example, perhaps you have written a letter addressed to Mr. Smith, and you've named that file SMITH.LTR. You want to use that same letter and send it to Ms. Jones. With the Save **A**s command, you can change the address to "Ms. Jones," and save the slightly-altered file under a new name, while still retaining the original SMITH.LTR file.

To use the Save **A**s command:

1. Click on **F**ile, or press **Alt+F**.
2. Click on Save **A**s, or press **A**.
3. Enter the new file name.
4. Select **OK**.

TIP

Power Bar Shortcut   You can perform a quick save for a new document (or an existing document) by pressing the **Save** button on the Power Bar. If the document is new, the Save As dialog box will appear, and you can name your file. If the document has been saved before, WordPerfect for Windows saves it automatically, and nothing appears on your screen.

OPENING A DOCUMENT

Why Open a Document?

Unless you plan to create new documents every time you work with WordPerfect, it's a good idea to learn how to open the documents you've saved. The **Open** command, located in the **File** menu, allows you to open files you have previously worked on, as well as files from other directories.

When you use the **Open** command, a dialog box appears, with a list of files to open. WordPerfect displays the **c:\wpwin60\wpdocs** directory automatically when you select the **Open** command. You can change directories, locate specific file names, display file types, and change drives. Once you've found the file you're looking for, you can open it and begin working on it again.

Type the name of the file you want to open in the Filename text box.

Directories list box

Command buttons

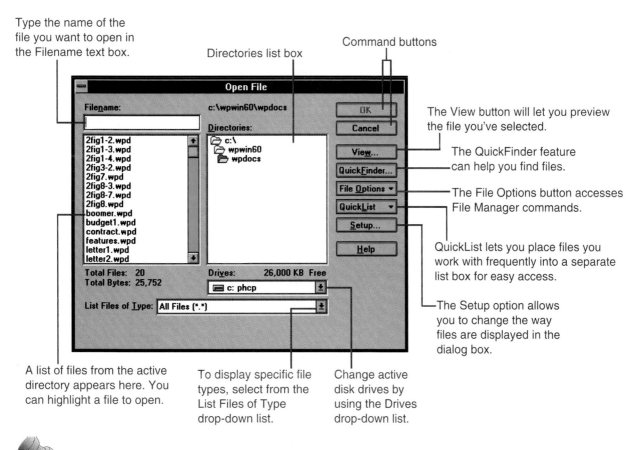

The View button will let you preview the file you've selected.

The QuickFinder feature can help you find files.

The File Options button accesses File Manager commands.

QuickList lets you place files you work with frequently into a separate list box for easy access.

The Setup option allows you to change the way files are displayed in the dialog box.

A list of files from the active directory appears here. You can highlight a file to open.

To display specific file types, select from the List Files of Type drop-down list.

Change active disk drives by using the Drives drop-down list.

TIP

Opening Tip   When you open another file without closing the document you were working with, the new file appears in your document window. The old file is there, too—you just can't see it.

OPENING A DOCUMENT

Opening a Document

1 Click on **File**, or press **Alt+F**.

2 Click on **Open**, or press **O**.

3 Select a file name from the list box, or type in the name of the file to be opened.

4 Click on **OK**, or press **Enter**.

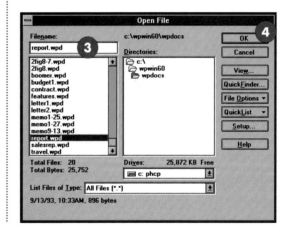

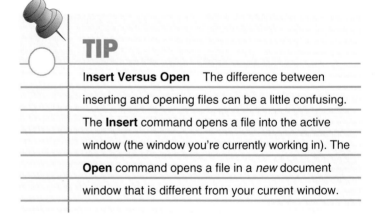

TIP

Insert Versus Open   The difference between inserting and opening files can be a little confusing. The **Insert** command opens a file into the active window (the window you're currently working in). The **Open** command opens a file in a *new* document window that is different from your current window.

TIP

Inserting a Document   Often you'll want to find a document you've worked on previously, and bring it into the current document window. This is called *inserting*. WordPerfect for Windows uses the Insert File command to insert documents into your current document window. WordPerfect goes to the **c:\wpwin60\wpdocs** directory automatically when you select the Insert File command. A dialog box appears, listing the files in the current directory. Once you've found the file you're looking for, you can bring it into your current document window, and place it wherever the cursor is located.

1. Click on Insert, or press **Alt+I**.

2. Click on File, or press **I**.

Insert	
Bullets & Numbers...	
Character...	Ctrl+W
Abbreviations...	
Date	▶
Other	▶
Footnote	▶
Endnote	▶
Comment	▶
Sound...	
Bookmark...	
Spreadsheet/Database	▶
File...	
Object...	
Page Break	Ctrl+Enter

3. Select a file name from the list box, or type in the name of the file to be inserted.

4. Click on the Insert button, or press **Enter**.

Insert File

Filename: budget1.wpd

c:\wpwin60\wpdocs

Directories:
c:\
 wpwin60
  wpdocs

2fig1-2.wpd
2fig1-3.wpd
2fig1-4.wpd
2fig3-2.wpd
2fig7.wpd
2fig8-3.wpd
2fig8-7.wpd
2fig8.wpd
boomer.wpd
budget1.wpd
contract.wpd
features.wpd
letter1.wpd
letter2.wpd

Total Files: 20
Total Bytes: 25,752

Drives: 25,808 KB Free
c: phcp

List Files of Type: All Files (*.*)

9/13/93, 10:33AM, 896 bytes

Insert
Cancel
View...
QuickFinder...
File Options ▼
QuickList ▼
Setup...
Help

5. Click on Yes, or press **Enter**.

FINDING AND REPLACING TEXT

Why Find and Replace Text?

When working with documents, sometimes you may need to locate a particular word or phrase and replace it with something else. WordPerfect for Windows features a convenient way of searching through your text, without scrolling endlessly and reading every paragraph. The **Find** command and the **Replace** command can make your search painless.

The **Find** command, found in the Edit menu, quickly locates words or phrases. You can control how the search is conducted, whether WordPerfect looks for upper- or lowercase letters, or even what fonts the search includes. There are pull-down menus in the Find Text dialog box that provide options for your search.

The **Replace** command not only finds words or phrases, but also replaces them with new text. You can control whether a single text entry is replaced, or every occurence in the entire document. Use the pull-down menus in the Find and Replace Text dialog box to select options.

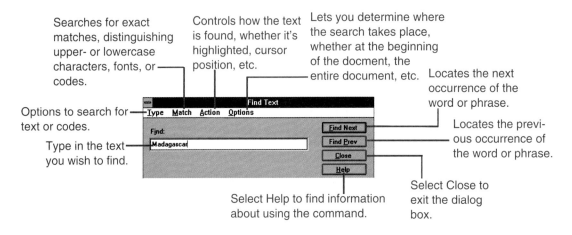

Searches for exact matches, distinguishing upper- or lowercase characters, fonts, or codes.

Controls how the text is found, whether it's highlighted, cursor position, etc.

Lets you determine where the search takes place, whether at the beginning of the docment, the entire document, etc.

Locates the next occurrence of the word or phrase.

Options to search for text or codes.

Type in the text you wish to find.

Locates the previous occurrence of the word or phrase.

Select Help to find information about using the command.

Select Close to exit the dialog box.

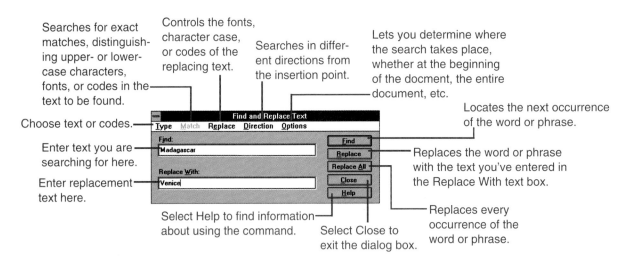

Searches for exact matches, distinguishing upper- or lowercase characters, fonts, or codes in the text to be found.

Controls the fonts, character case, or codes of the replacing text.

Searches in different directions from the insertion point.

Lets you determine where the search takes place, whether at the beginning of the docment, the entire document, etc.

Locates the next occurrence of the word or phrase.

Choose text or codes.

Enter text you are searching for here.

Enter replacement text here.

Replaces the word or phrase with the text you've entered in the Replace With text box.

Replaces every occurrence of the word or phrase.

Select Help to find information about using the command.

Select Close to exit the dialog box.

Finding Text

1 Click on **Edit**, or press **Alt+E**.

2 Click on Find, or press **F**.

3 Type in the word or phrase you wish to search for.

4 Select any menu options you wish to use in your search.

5 Click the command buttons to begin your search.

6 Click **Close**, or press **C** to exit the dialog box.

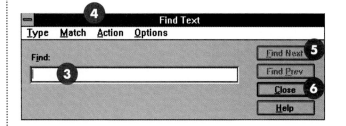

TIP

Dialog Box Shortcuts   Press **F2** to display the Find Text dialog box quickly. Press **Ctrl+F2** to display the Find and Replace Text Dialog Box.

Creating, Editing, Saving, and Printing Documents

FINDING AND REPLACING TEXT

Finding and Replacing Text

1 Click on **Edit**, or press **Alt+E**.

2 Click on **Replace**, or press **R**.

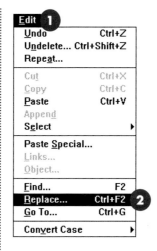

3 Type in the word or phrase you wish to search for.

4 Type in the replacement text.

5 Select any menu options you wish to use in your search.

6 Click on the command buttons to begin your search and replace.

7 Click on **Close**, or press **Alt+C** to exit the dialog box.

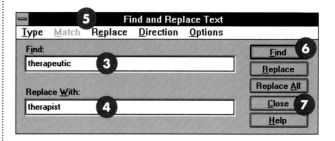

TIP

Search and Replace Tips You can highlight a word or phrase before using the **Find** and **Replace** commands, and avoid the step of typing text into the dialog text box.

When you use the **Replace All** command, a dialog box will appear after the command has been executed, verifying the replacement has occurred. Click **OK** or press **Enter**.

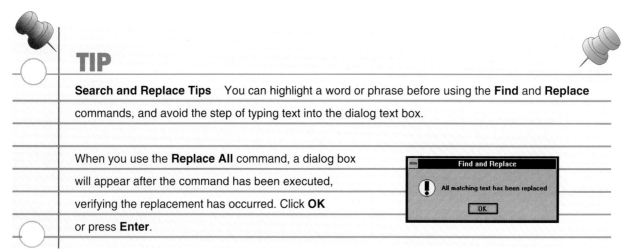

ZOOMING IN AND OUT

What Is a Zoom?

The **Zoom** feature allows you to change the way you look at your document. You can zoom in for a closer look (based on percentages of actual size) at your document's details. Or you can zoom out to see the entire document page.

Zooming in and out is a handy way of previewing what your document will look like before it's printed. It also helps you gauge how the layout looks, and check to see if everything is placed where you want it.

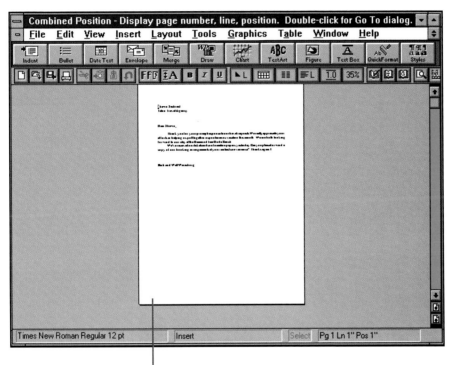

A full-page zoom lets you see the entire document.

ZOOMING IN AND OUT

Zooming

1 Click View, or press **Alt+V**.

2 Click on Zoom, or press **Z**.

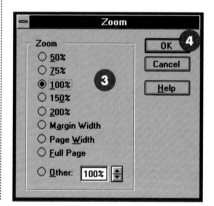

3 Select the perspective in which you wish to see the document.

4 Click on **OK**, or press **Enter**.

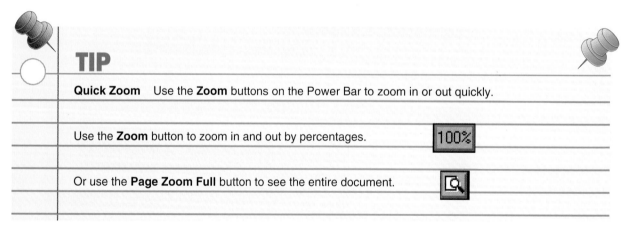

TIP

Quick Zoom   Use the **Zoom** buttons on the Power Bar to zoom in or out quickly.

Use the **Zoom** button to zoom in and out by percentages.

Or use the **Page Zoom Full** button to see the entire document.

WORKING WITH MULTIPLE DOCUMENTS

Why Work with *Multiple* Documents?

A great advantage of WordPerfect for Windows 6.0 is the ability to work with more than one document at a time. You can open and work on a new file while the previous file you were using is still open. This makes moving and copying text from one file to another a very simple task to do.

Best of all, you can display your multiple documents on one screen, all at the same time. This allows you to see into several documents at once. The document you are currently working in has a highlighted Title bar, indicating the window is *active*. The Windows menu has two arrangements you can use to display your multiple documents, *Tile* and *Cascade*.

The Cascade option will stagger the documents across the screen, overlapping the document windows.

Control-menu box

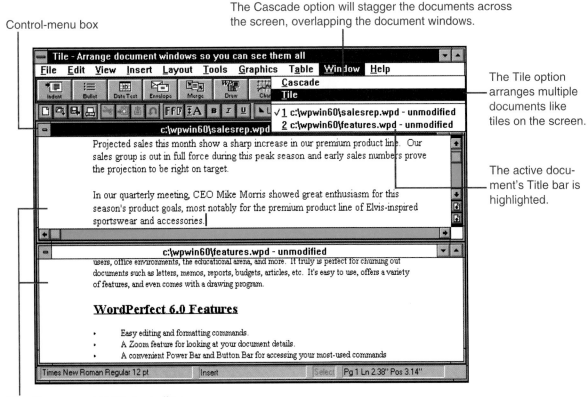

The Tile option arranges multiple documents like tiles on the screen.

The active document's Title bar is highlighted.

Two files opened at the same time.

WORKING WITH MULTIPLE DOCUMENTS

Arranging Multiple Documents on Your Screen

❶ Make sure two document files are opened. Click on **Window**, or press **Alt+W**.

❷ Choose which display arrangement to use to display your open document windows. Click with the mouse, or highlight with the **arrow** keys and press **Enter**.

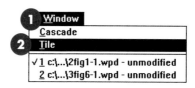

LEARNING THE LINGO

Active document: The document you are working on currently, indicated by a highlighted Title bar. When more than one document is opened, you can work on only one at a time.

Tile: Arranging multiple document windows into squares on the screen.

Cascade: Arranging multiple document windows so that they overlap and their Title bars are visible.

QUICK REFRESHER

When you open another file without closing the document you were working with, the new file appears in your document window. The old file is there, too—you just can't see it.

To open another file on top of your current file, follow these steps:

1. With a document open in the document window, click on **F**ile or press **Alt+F**.

2. Click on **O**pen, or press **O**.

3. The Open File dialog box will appear. Select another file to open, then click on **OK** or press **Enter**.

TIP

Changing Active Windows and Moving Them Around   You can make an open window active by clicking anywhere inside the window. Remember, the active window will always have a highlighted Title bar. You can also move your multiple windows around on-screen. Just move the mouse pointer to the Title bar of the window you want to move, then press the left mouse button and drag the window to a new position. Release the button, and you're relocated your window!

TIP

Switcheroo When working with several open documents that are not all displayed on the screen at the same time, use the **Windows** menu to switch easily from one open document window to another.

1. Click on **W**indow, or press **Alt+W**.
2. At the bottom of the menu is a list of opened files.

A checkmark denotes which file is the active document.

To switch from one to another, click on the file name

(or highlight with the arrow keys) and press **Enter**.

Window
Cascade
Tile
1 c:\...\2fig1-1.wpd - unmodified
√2 c:\...\3fig6-1.wpd - unmodified

TIP

Closing a Document To close a document at any time:

1. Click on **F**ile, or press **Alt+F**.
2. Click on **C**lose, or press **C**.

You can also double-click on the document's Control-menu box to close.

TIP

Copying or Moving Text Between Windows

Select the text to be copied or moved. Press **Ctrl+Insert** to copy; press **Shift+Delete** to move. Move the cursor to the document into which you want to insert the text. Press **Shift+Insert**. You can also use the **E**dit **C**opy and Edit Cu**t** commands, then **P**aste.

Creating, Editing, Saving, and Printing Documents

PRINTING A DOCUMENT

When Can a Document Be Printed?

You can print a document at any time, but ordinarily you'll want to print it after you've completed work on it. It's a good idea to preview your document before you print it out, so you can make sure everything looks the way you want it to. Take a look at the "Zooming In and Out" task earlier in this section.

When you're finally ready to print, use the **File Print** command. The Print dialog box will appear, offering you many printing options. You can control how many copies are printed, print quality, and more.

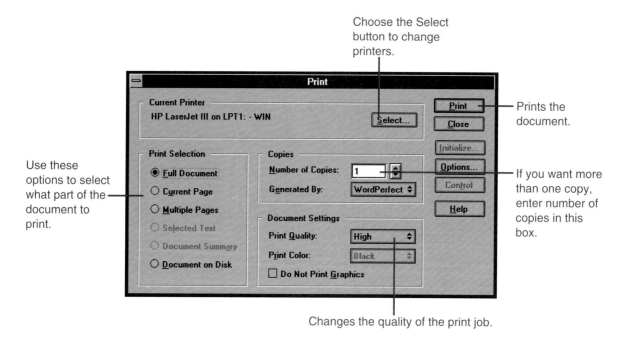

Choose the Select button to change printers.

Prints the document.

Use these options to select what part of the document to print.

If you want more than one copy, enter number of copies in this box.

Changes the quality of the print job.

Printing

1 Click on **File**, or press **Alt+F**.

2 Click on **Print**, or press **P**.

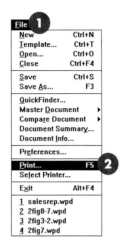

3 Change printing options (as desired) in the Print dialog box.

4 When ready to print, click on Print or press **P**.

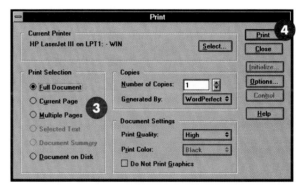

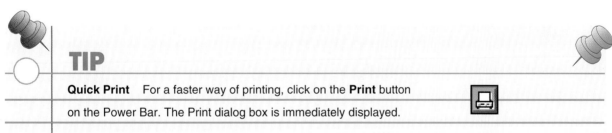

TIP

Quick Print For a faster way of printing, click on the **Print** button on the Power Bar. The Print dialog box is immediately displayed.

Creating, Editing, Saving, and Printing Documents

PART 3

Enhancing Your Document

In this section, you'll learn the various techniques for improving your document, and the steps to making things look just the way you want.

You'll learn about:

- Enhancing Text
- Viewing WordPerfect for Windows Codes
- Displaying the Ruler
- Setting Margins
- Setting Tabs
- Indenting Text
- Choosing a Justification Style
- Adding Headers and Footers
- Creating Tables
- Using the Spell Checker
- Using the Thesaurus
- Using the Grammar Checker
- Using the Drawing Program

ENHANCING TEXT

What Is a Text Enhancement?

A *text enhancement*, also called *formatting*, is a characteristic or style that is applied to text, such as italics or bold. Text enhancements can be used to make characters, words, or paragraphs stand out to improve the look of your document. Text enhancements include different fonts, point sizes, underlines, and more.

You can change the look of your text before you begin typing, after you're finished with the document, or even right in the middle of your document. You can apply text enhancements to a single character, a word, a paragraph, or an entire document. Text enhancements can be activated with the **Font** command and the Font dialog box. Common text enhancements are also available on the Power Bar.

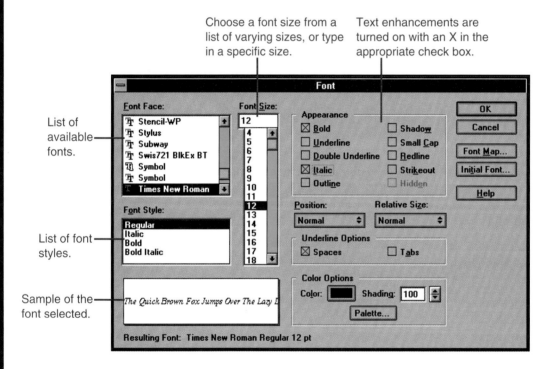

Choose a font size from a list of varying sizes, or type in a specific size.

Text enhancements are turned on with an X in the appropriate check box.

List of available fonts.

List of font styles.

Sample of the font selected.

LEARNING THE LINGO

Text Enhancements: A characteristic, such as italics, that is applied to text.

Formatting: Changing the look of text or positioning of text in a document.

Font: A set of characters that share a particular design style.

Point Size: Text characters are measured in points, one point equals 1/72 inch.

Enhancing Text

1 If you want to change existing text, select text to be formatted.

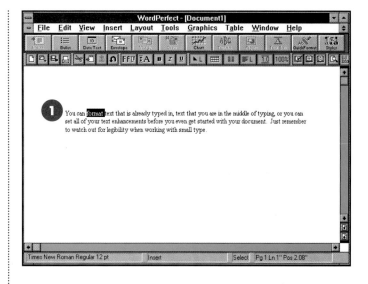

2 Click on **Layout**, or press **Alt+L**.

3 Click on **Font**, or press **F**.

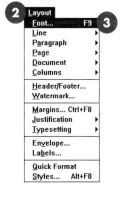

4 Select the text enhancements you wish to apply.

5 Click on **OK**, or press **Enter**.

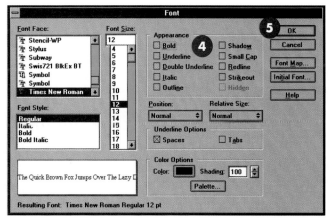

75

Enhancing Your Document

ENHANCING TEXT

Exercise

Type in the text shown, and practice formatting with the steps below.

1 Select the phrase "True West: A History of Pioneering" in the first sentence.

2 Change the font to Helvetica or another style.

3 Change the formatting to bold, underline.

4 Select the word "really" in the first sentence.

5 Change the formatting to italic.

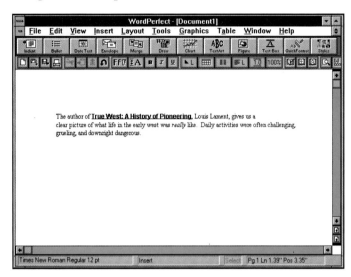

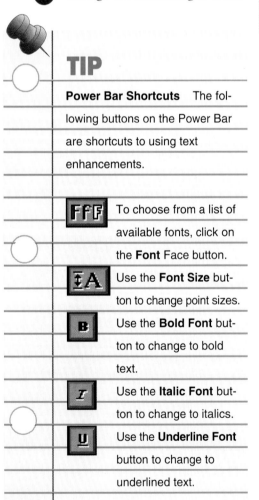

TIP

Power Bar Shortcuts   The following buttons on the Power Bar are shortcuts to using text enhancements.

To choose from a list of available fonts, click on the **Font** Face button.

Use the **Font Size** button to change point sizes.

Use the **Bold Font** button to change to bold text.

Use the **Italic Font** button to change to italics.

Use the **Underline Font** button to change to underlined text.

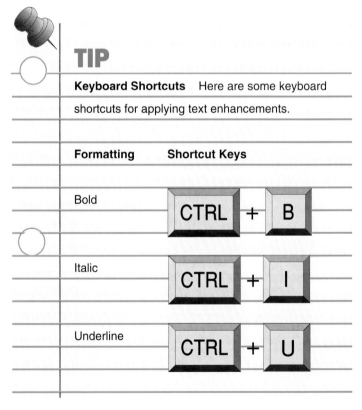

TIP

Keyboard Shortcuts   Here are some keyboard shortcuts for applying text enhancements.

Formatting	Shortcut Keys
Bold	CTRL + B
Italic	CTRL + I
Underline	CTRL + U

VIEWING WORDPERFECT FOR WINDOWS CODES

What Are Codes?

When you add text enhancements and formatting to your document, WordPerfect keeps track of those features with *special codes*. For example, when you set a paragraph in italics, WordPerfect for Windows 6.0 will insert an **Italics On** code at the beginning of the paragraph, and an **Italics Off** code at the end of the paragraph. These codes resemble little sales-tags in shape, or boxes that look like buttons.

Normally, you will not be able to see these codes. However, on occasion it will be necessary to view the codes—for instance, if you insert a code that doesn't seem to be working. Usually this happens because an existing code is already in place, and the new code is being ignored. To fix the situation, you'll need to see the WordPerfect for Windows codes. You can edit them if necessary.

When the codes are displayed, WordPerfect for Windows splits the document window, showing the normal document in the top half, and the document with codes revealed in the bottom half. You can type, make changes, and move around in the bottom half of the screen, just as you would in the normal screen. Whatever changes you make are made to both screen halves. Sometimes being able to edit the codes as you see them can save you time.

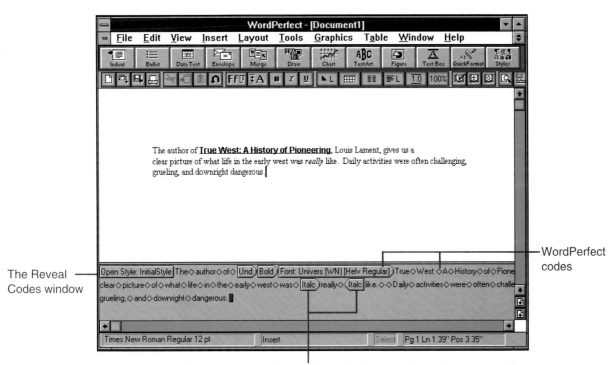

The Reveal Codes window

WordPerfect codes

Some codes are inserted as pairs that turn formatting on and off.

Enhancing Your Document

VIEWING WORDPERFECT FOR WINDOWS CODES

Displaying and Hiding Codes

1 To display or hide codes, click on View or press **Alt+V**.

2 Click on Reveal Codes, or press **C**. A checkmark next to the command name indicates the codes will be revealed. If there's no checkmark, the codes will be hidden.

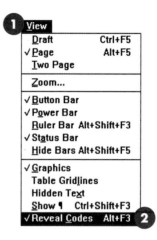

LEARNING THE LINGO

Special Codes: Formatting codes WordPerfect for Windows 6.0 places within your document to indicate where the formatting begins and ends.

TIP

Editing Codes   Editing the codes themselves can sometimes save you time. For example, if you wanted to remove the bold formatting from a paragraph, you would normally have to select the paragraph, then select the menu command or the shortcut button to remove the bold enhancement. However, with Reveal **C**odes, you can get rid of the bold by deleting the code with a single keystroke. In the Reveal **C**odes window, simply place the cursor on the code you want to remove, then press the **Delete** key. If the code is a *paired code* (one that's turned on and off), just delete one of the pair and WordPerfect will remove the other.

DISPLAYING THE RULER

What Do You Do with the Ruler?

The Ruler Bar can help you set margins and tabs, format paragraphs, and set up tables and columns in your document. When you start WordPerfect for Windows 6.0, the Ruler Bar does not appear. However, it can easily be added to your document by opening the **View** menu and selecting **Ruler Bar**.

When visible, the Ruler Bar appears below the Power Bar at the top of your document. To learn how to use the ruler, turn to the "Setting Margins" and "Setting Tabs" tasks later in this section.

The top portion of the ruler controls margins.

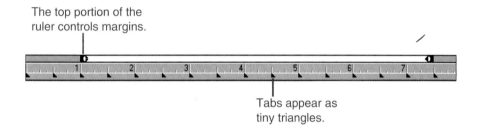

Tabs appear as tiny triangles.

Displaying and Hiding the Ruler

1 To display or hide the ruler, click on View or press **Alt+V**.

2 Click on **Ruler Bar**, or press **R**. A checkmark next to the command name indicates the ruler will be visible. If there's no checkmark, the ruler will be hidden.

View **1**
_D_raft	Ctrl+F5
√_P_age	Alt+F5
_T_wo Page	
_Z_oom...	
√_B_utton Bar	
√P_o_wer Bar	
√_R_uler Bar	Alt+Shift+F3 **2**
√S_t_atus Bar	
_H_ide Bars	Alt+Shift+F5
√_G_raphics	
Hidden Te_x_t	
_S_how ¶	Ctrl+Shift+F3
Reveal _C_odes	Alt+F3

TIP

Ruler Features   Click the right mouse button on the Ruler to display a QuickMenu listing features you can access with the Ruler Bar.

LEARNING THE LINGO

Margin: The space between your text and the outer edge of your page.

Tab: A keystroke that moves text to a specified point in your document. Tabs are used to align text.

Enhancing Your Document

79

SETTING MARGINS

What Are Margins and How Do You Use Them?

Margins are the edges of white space that border your document. WordPerfect for Windows 6.0 uses a default margin of 1 inch all around. In most cases, the default margins are fine, but you can easily adjust the margin to your own document's needs when necessary.

Margins can be changed using the Margin command from the **Layout** menu. You can control all four margin sides of your document independently. You can also use the Ruler Bar to set margins (a Tip in this task will give you details).

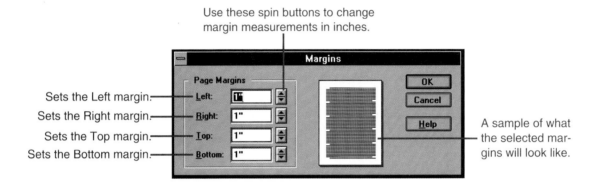

Use these spin buttons to change margin measurements in inches.

Sets the Left margin.
Sets the Right margin.
Sets the Top margin.
Sets the Bottom margin.

A sample of what the selected margins will look like.

LEARNING THE LINGO

Margin: The space between your text and the outer edge of your page.

TIP

Quick Margin Display   To display the Margin dialog box quickly, double-click on a margin marker in the Ruler Bar.

TIP

Multiple Margins   You can change margins throughout your document. New margin settings can be applied to a single line, a paragraph, or large groups of text blocks. Select the text block to be affected, then follow the steps for setting the margins with the Margin command.

Setting Margins with the Margin Command

1 Click on **Layout**, or press **Alt+L**.

2 Click on **Margins**, or press **M**.

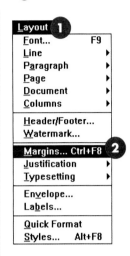

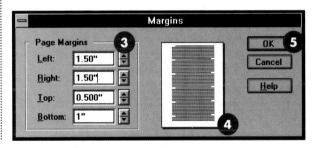

3 Adjust the margin settings using the spin buttons.

4 Preview the new margins by checking the sample.

5 Click on **OK**, or press **Enter**.

TIP

Setting Margins with the Ruler Bar For a quick margin adjustment, use the Ruler Bar. (See the "Displaying the Ruler" task to find out how the Ruler is displayed.)

Click and hold on the left or right margin marker, depending on which margin is to be changed, then drag the margin marker to its new position. Release the mouse button when the margin marker is in its new place.

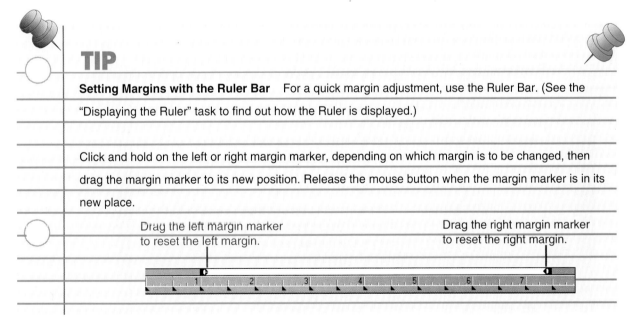

Drag the left margin marker to reset the left margin.

Drag the right margin marker to reset the right margin.

Enhancing Your Document

SETTING TABS

What Are Tabs and How Do They Work?

Tabs are used to align text. Tabs can indent a single line, or line up whole columns of text. There are eight tab types in WordPerfect: Left, Right, Center, Decimal, and four types of Dot Leader tabs. WordPerfect for Windows is set up with default left tabs set 1/2-inch apart.

Tabs can be changed using the **Tab Set** command. You can control types of tabs, placement of tabs, and how they affect text. You can also use the Ruler Bar to set tabs.

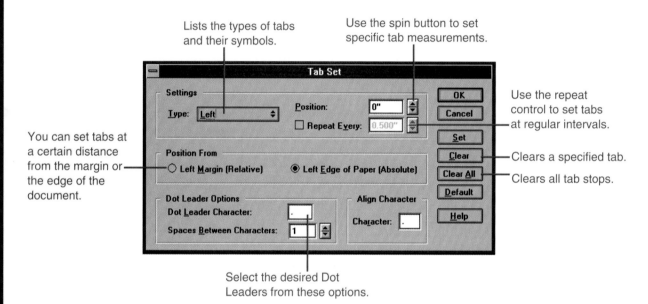

Lists the types of tabs and their symbols.

Use the spin button to set specific tab measurements.

Use the repeat control to set tabs at regular intervals.

Clears a specified tab.

Clears all tab stops.

You can set tabs at a certain distance from the margin or the edge of the document.

Select the desired Dot Leaders from these options.

Types of Tabs

Tab icon	Tab type	How it affects text
◣	Left tab	Left edge of text aligns at tab stop.
◢	Right tab	Right edge of text aligns at tab stop.
▲	Center tab	Centers text at tab stop.
⬥	Decimal tab	Text appearing before the decimal point aligns to the left of tab stop, text following decimal point aligns to the right of the tab stop. Decimals are perfectly aligned.
◣ ◢ ▲ ▲	Dot Leaders	Characters, such as hyphens or dots, fill the tab space between words.

82

Setting Tabs with the Tab Command

1 Click on Layout, or press **Alt+L**.

2 Click on Line, or press **L**.

3 Click on Tab Set, or press **T**.

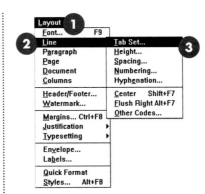

4 Select the tab type from the Type list options.

5 Select tab position with the Position spin buttons.

6 Click on **OK**, or press **Enter**.

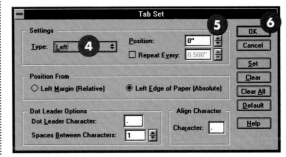

LEARNING THE LINGO

Tab: A keystroke that moves text to a specified point in your document. Tabs are used to align text.

TIP

Quick Tabs   To access the Tab symbols quickly, use the **Tab Set** button on the Power Bar.

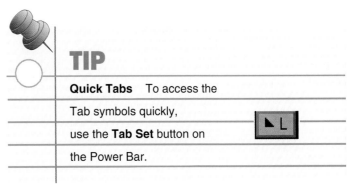

TIP

Tab Tabs   You can change tabs throughout your document. New tab stops can be applied to a single line, a paragraph, or large groups of text blocks. Place the cursor where the tab is to be applied, or select the text block that has tabs. Insert a new tab stop on the Ruler Bar by following the steps in the "Setting Tabs with the Ruler Bar" Tip in this task.

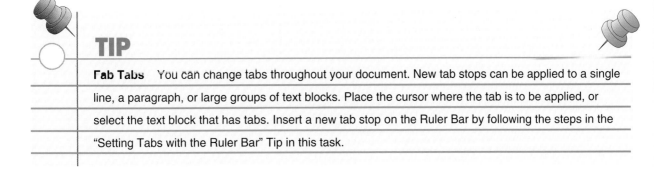

Enhancing Your Document

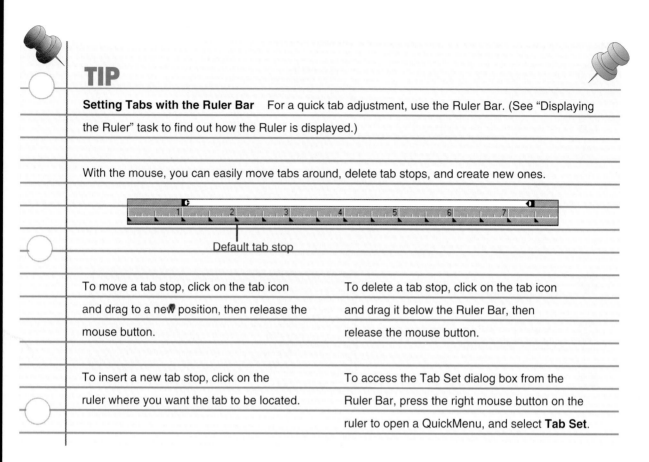

TIP

Setting Tabs with the Ruler Bar For a quick tab adjustment, use the Ruler Bar. (See "Displaying the Ruler" task to find out how the Ruler is displayed.)

With the mouse, you can easily move tabs around, delete tab stops, and create new ones.

Default tab stop

To move a tab stop, click on the tab icon and drag to a new position, then release the mouse button.

To delete a tab stop, click on the tab icon and drag it below the Ruler Bar, then release the mouse button.

To insert a new tab stop, click on the ruler where you want the tab to be located.

To access the Tab Set dialog box from the Ruler Bar, press the right mouse button on the ruler to open a QuickMenu, and select **Tab Set**.

INDENTING TEXT

Why Indent Text?

Indents are used to place extra distance between text and margins. Indents can set off a block of text within your document, draw attention to special paragraphs for emphasis, and improve the overall look of your document.

You can indent a line, a block of text, a paragraph, or an entire document. Each time you indent, text moves over by one tab stop. You can indent before you start typing, or after text is entered.

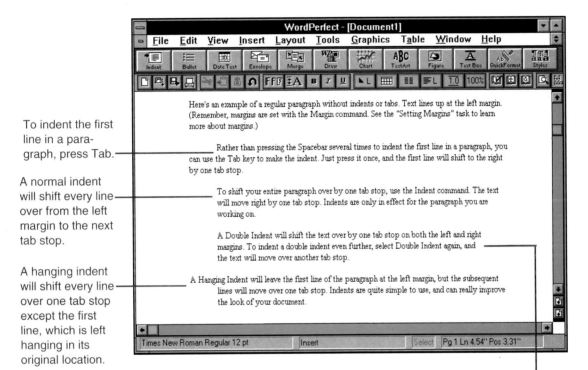

To indent the first line in a paragraph, press Tab.

A normal indent will shift every line over from the left margin to the next tab stop.

A hanging indent will shift every line over one tab stop except the first line, which is left hanging in its original location.

A double indent will move every line over one tab stop on both the left and right margins.

LEARNING THE LINGO

Indent: Shifting text away from the margins.

Indenting Text

1 Place the cursor where text is to be indented.

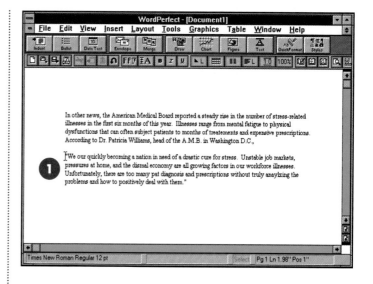

2 Click on **Layout**, or press **Alt+L**.

3 Click on **Paragraph**, or press **P**.

4 Choose an indent.

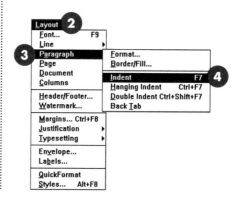

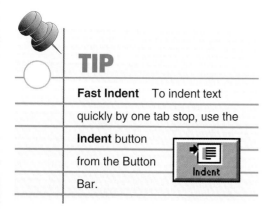

TIP

Fast Indent   To indent text quickly by one tab stop, use the **Indent** button from the Button Bar.

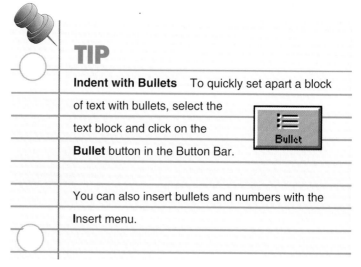

TIP

Indent with Bullets   To quickly set apart a block of text with bullets, select the text block and click on the **Bullet** button in the Button Bar.

You can also insert bullets and numbers with the Insert menu.

CHOOSING A JUSTIFICATION STYLE

What Is Justification?

Justification, or *alignment*, refers to the way text is positioned between the left and right margins in your WordPerfect for Windows document. Alignment means that the edges of your text line up. WordPerfect for Windows aligns text to the left automatically when you open a document. However, text can also be aligned to the right, centered between both margins, or fully justified—aligned at both the left and right margins.

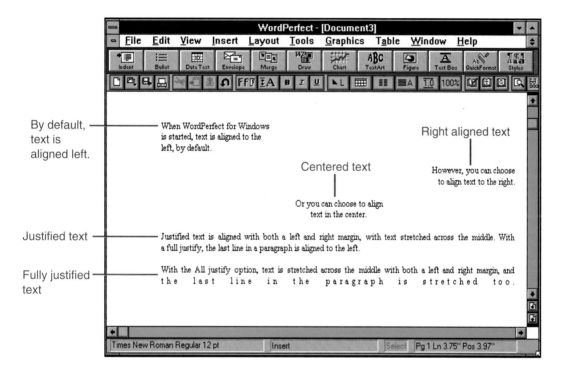

By default, text is aligned left.

Justified text

Fully justified text

LEARNING THE LINGO

Justification: The positioning of text within a document in regard to the left and right margins. Also called alignment.

CHOOSING A JUSTIFICATION STYLE

Aligning Text

1 Position the cursor where text is to be entered, or select the text to be aligned.

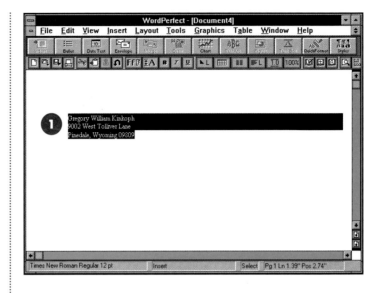

2 Click on **Layout**, or press **Alt+L**.

3 Click on **Justification**, or press **J**.

4 Select the type of alignment to apply.

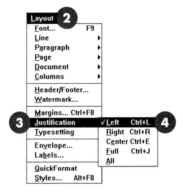

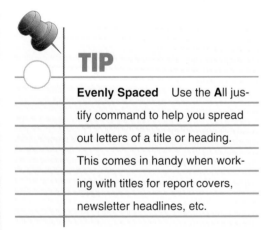

TIP

Evenly Spaced   Use the **All** justify command to help you spread out letters of a title or heading. This comes in handy when working with titles for report covers, newsletter headlines, etc.

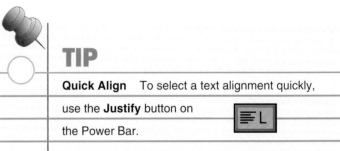

TIP

Quick Align   To select a text alignment quickly, use the **Justify** button on the Power Bar.

Exercise

Type in the following three text blocks, and follow these steps to practice aligning.

1 Select the text block.

2 Click on **Layout**, or press **Alt+L**.

3 Click on **Justification**, or press **J**.

4 Select **Right** to align text at right margin.

5 Select the second text block.

6 Click on **Layout**, or press **Alt+L**.

7 Click on **Justification**, or press **J**.

8 Select **Full** to align text at both margins.

9 Select the third text block.

10 Click on **Layout**, or press **Alt+L**.

11 Click on **Justification**, or press **J**.

12 Select **Center** to center text between both margins.

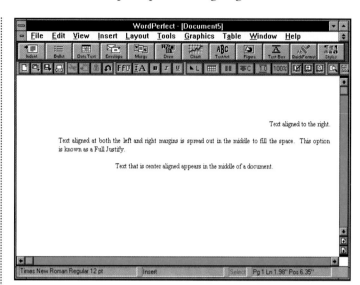

CHOOSING A JUSTIFICATION STYLE

TIP

The Line Spacing Command   Along with indents and justification, you can also control the vertical spacing of your text. The **Line Spacing** command controls the space between lines. For example, a measurement of 1.0 places one extra line space between lines, 2.0 is a double space, etc.

To use the **Line Spacing** command, follow these steps:

1. Click on **L**ayout, or press **Alt+L**.

2. Click on **L**ine, or press **L**.

3. Click on **S**pacing, or press **S**.

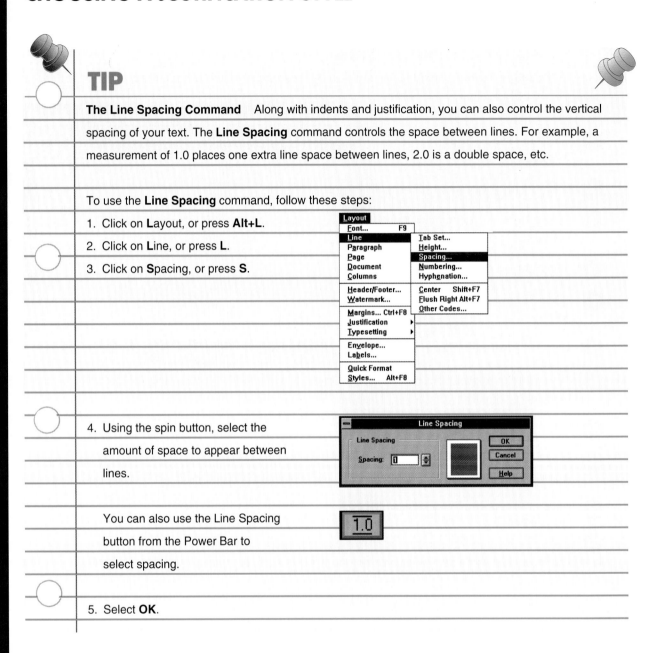

4. Using the spin button, select the amount of space to appear between lines.

You can also use the Line Spacing button from the Power Bar to select spacing.

5. Select **OK**.

ADDING HEADERS AND FOOTERS

What Are Headers and Footers?

Headers and *footers* are used to place information at the top or bottom of a document page, such as a chapter title or a company name and address, that will be repeated on every page when printed. A *header* is text at the top of a page, a *footer* is text at the bottom. Headers and footers can be set up to repeat on every page or alternating pages.

After selecting the **Header/Footer** command and type of header or footer, a *Feature Bar* appears on screen. Header and footer options can be selected from the Control Bar, and the text is typed in. After entering text and options, you can close the Header/Footer Feature Bar and the header or footer will appear on your printed document.

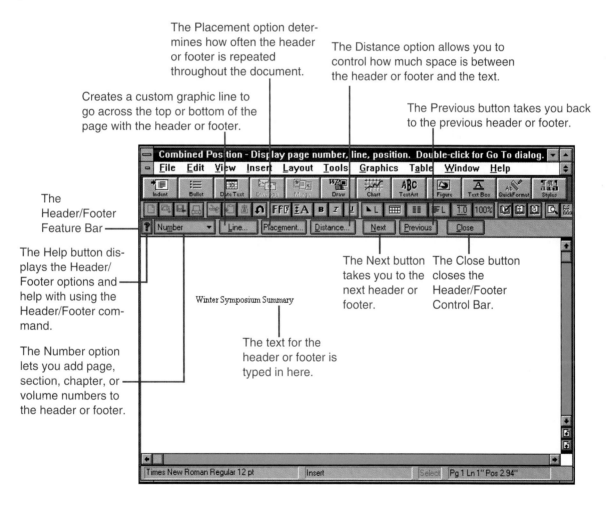

The Placement option determines how often the header or footer is repeated throughout the document.

The Distance option allows you to control how much space is between the header or footer and the text.

Creates a custom graphic line to go across the top or bottom of the page with the header or footer.

The Previous button takes you back to the previous header or footer.

The Header/Footer Feature Bar

The Help button displays the Header/Footer options and help with using the Header/Footer command.

The Number option lets you add page, section, chapter, or volume numbers to the header or footer.

The Next button takes you to the next header or footer.

The Close button closes the Header/Footer Control Bar.

The text for the header or footer is typed in here.

Winter Symposium Summary

Enhancing Your Document

ADDING HEADERS AND FOOTERS

Creating a Header or Footer

1 Click on **Layout** or press **Alt+L**.

2 Click on **Header/Footer**, or press **H**.

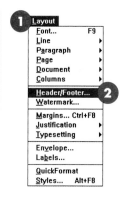

3 Select header or footer type from the option buttons.

4 Click on **Create**, or press **Enter**.

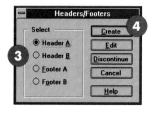

5 Type in the header or footer text.

6 Select options from the Header/Footer Feature Bar.

7 Click on **Close**, or press **Alt+Shift+C** to close the Header/Footer Control Bar.

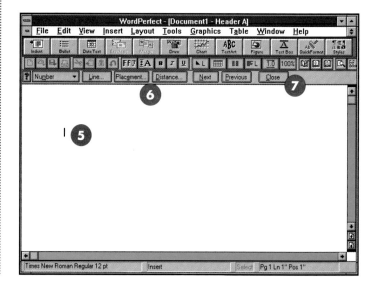

TIP

Keyboard Tips To select the Header/Footer Feature Bar buttons with the keyboard, press **Alt+Shift** plus the selection letter of the option you wish to choose.

LEARNING THE LINGO

Header: Text that is repeated at the top of every page or alternating pages. Headers can include report titles, company name, dates, etc.

Footer: Text that is repeated at the bottom of every page or alternating pages. Footers can include chapter titles, file names, dates, etc.

Feature Bar: A special bar of options that appears below the Power Bar when working with headers and footers.

TIP

Deleting a Header or Footer   To delete a header or footer, follow these steps:

1. Click on **L**ayout or press **Alt+L**.

2. Click on **H**eader/Footer, or press **H**.

3. Select the header or footer you want to delete.

4. Select **D**iscontinue.

To remove the Header/Footer Feature Bar from your screen, click **C**lose or press **Alt+Shift+C**.

Enhancing Your Document

CREATING TABLES

Why Make a Table?

Tables are another way to display information in your document. Tables are made up of rows and columns. Each segment inside the table is called a *cell*. Use tables to help organize document information, facts, and figures.

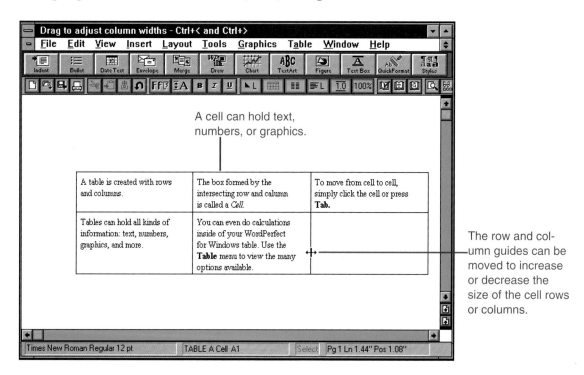

A cell can hold text, numbers, or graphics.

A table is created with rows and columns.	The box formed by the intersecting row and column is called a *Cell*.	To move from cell to cell, simply click the cell or press **Tab.**
Tables can hold all kinds of information: text, numbers, graphics, and more.	You can even do calculations inside of your WordPerfect for Windows table. Use the **Table** menu to view the many options available.	

The row and column guides can be moved to increase or decrease the size of the cell rows or columns.

LEARNING THE LINGO

Table: A chart of information arranged in rows and columns.

Cell: A section in a table where information is typed. Cells usually resemble the shape of a box.

Creating a Table

1 Place the cursor where the table is to be inserted in your document, then click on Table or press **Alt+A**.

2 Click on Create, or press **C**.

3 Select a table size in terms of columns and rows. Click the spin button to designate numbers, or type in the number of columns and rows.

4 Click **OK**, or press **Enter**.

5 Type in text for each cell as needed.

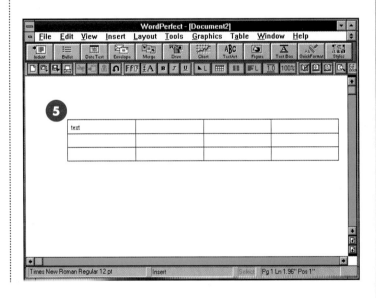

Enhancing Your Document

USING THE SPELL CHECKER

What Is a Spell Checker?

WordPerfect for Windows 6.0 features a *spell checker*—a handy tool for checking the spelling of your text, saving you time in proofreading your document. The Speller tool can quickly check the spelling of a word, a sentence, a paragraph, or an entire document. You'll find this tool an invaluable part of creating professional documents with WordPerfect.

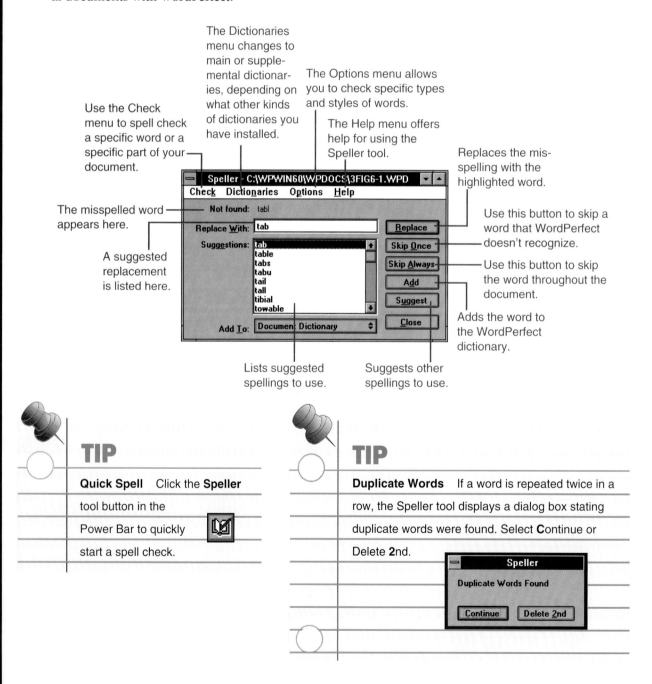

The Dictionaries menu changes to main or supplemental dictionaries, depending on what other kinds of dictionaries you have installed.

The Options menu allows you to check specific types and styles of words.

Use the Check menu to spell check a specific word or a specific part of your document.

The Help menu offers help for using the Speller tool.

Replaces the misspelling with the highlighted word.

The misspelled word appears here.

Use this button to skip a word that WordPerfect doesn't recognize.

A suggested replacement is listed here.

Use this button to skip the word throughout the document.

Adds the word to the WordPerfect dictionary.

Lists suggested spellings to use.

Suggests other spellings to use.

Speller - C:\WPWIN60\WPDOCS\3FIG6-1.WPD

Check   Dictionaries   Options   Help

Not found: tabl

Replace With: tab

Suggestions: tab / table / tabs / tabu / tail / tall / tibial / towable

Add To: Document Dictionary

Replace / Skip Once / Skip Always / Add / Suggest / Close

TIP

Quick Spell   Click the **Speller** tool button in the Power Bar to quickly start a spell check.

TIP

Duplicate Words   If a word is repeated twice in a row, the Speller tool displays a dialog box stating duplicate words were found. Select **C**ontinue or Delete **2**nd.

Speller

Duplicate Words Found

Continue / Delete 2nd

Using the Speller Tool

1 Move the cursor to the beginning of the document, then click on Tools, or press **Alt+T**.

2 Click on Speller, or press **S**.

3 To spell check your entire document immediately, click on Start or press **Enter**. To check a particular word, type in the word and look at the suggestions in the list box.

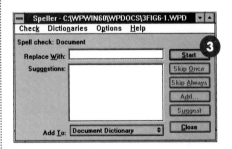

4 If a misspelled word is found, select an option to continue, or edit the word yourself by typing the change and selecting the **R**eplace button to continue.

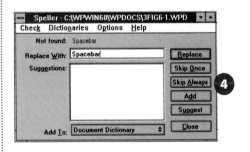

5 When the spell check is complete, a dialog box appears verifying the check. Click **Yes**, or press **Enter**.

USING THE THESAURUS

What Is the Thesaurus?

If you're having trouble coming up with a word that communicates what you intended, use the WordPerfect for Windows *Thesaurus* tool to help you out. The Thesaurus tool is a compilation of synonyms and antonyms that will help you perfect your document.

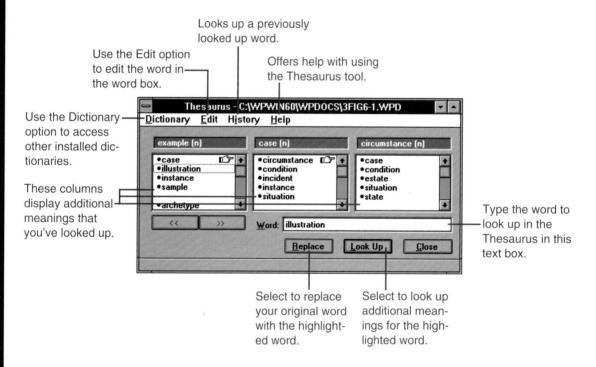

Looks up a previously looked up word.

Use the Edit option to edit the word in the word box.

Offers help with using the Thesaurus tool.

Use the Dictionary option to access other installed dictionaries.

These columns display additional meanings that you've looked up.

Type the word to look up in the Thesaurus in this text box.

Select to replace your original word with the highlighted word.

Select to look up additional meanings for the highlighted word.

LEARNING THE LINGO

Antonym: A word that means the opposite of another word.

Synonym: A word that means the same thing as another word.

Using the Thesaurus

1 Put the insertion point anywhere in the word you wish to look up.

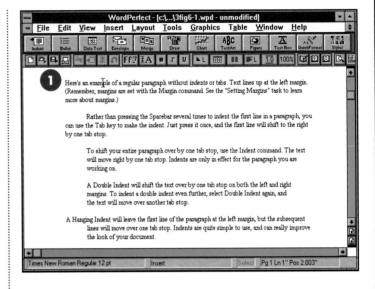

2 Click on **T**ools, or press **Alt+T**.

3 Click on **T**hesaurus, or press **T**.

4 Click on a replacement word from the list, or use the **arrow** keys to highlight it.

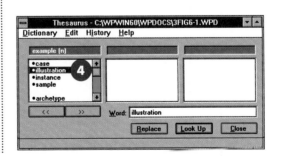

USING THE THESAURUS

5 To see additional words, click on **Look Up** and press **Enter**. Highlight the word you wish to use.

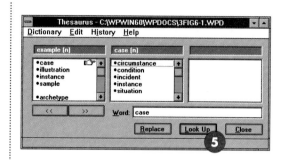

6 When you've found and highlighted the word to use, click on the **R**eplace button, or tab to the button and press **Enter**.

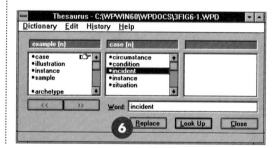

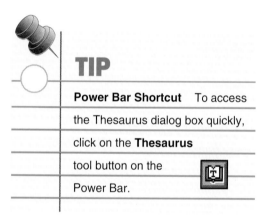

TIP

Power Bar Shortcut   To access the Thesaurus dialog box quickly, click on the **Thesaurus** tool button on the Power Bar.

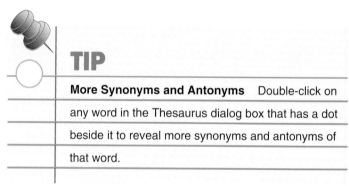

TIP

More Synonyms and Antonyms   Double-click on any word in the Thesaurus dialog box that has a dot beside it to reveal more synonyms and antonyms of that word.

USING THE GRAMMAR CHECKER

Why Check Your Grammar?

In the "Using the Spell Checker" task earlier in this section, you learned how to make WordPerfect for Windows 6.0 proofread your documents for spelling errors. But spelling errors aren't the only errors that occur in documents. Grammatical errors are also a problem—and the spell-checking tool doesn't look for grammatical errors, just spelling errors.

Thankfully, WordPerfect also comes with a *grammar checker* called ***Grammatik***. Grammatik searches your entire document for mistakes in grammar.

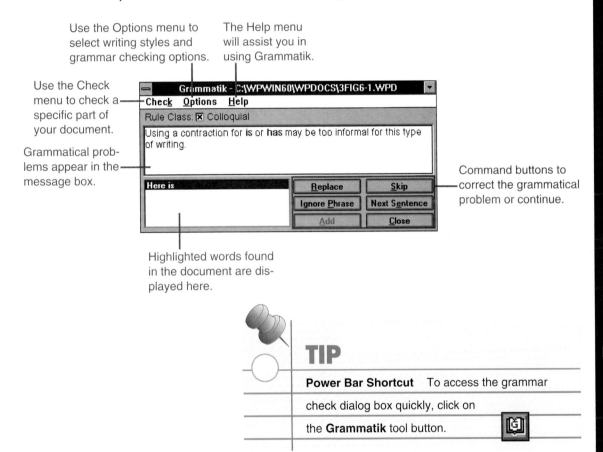

Use the Options menu to select writing styles and grammar checking options.

The Help menu will assist you in using Grammatik.

Use the Check menu to check a specific part of your document.

Grammatical problems appear in the message box.

Command buttons to correct the grammatical problem or continue.

Highlighted words found in the document are displayed here.

TIP

Power Bar Shortcut   To access the grammar check dialog box quickly, click on the **Grammatik** tool button.

Enhancing Your Document

USING THE GRAMMAR CHECKER

Checking Your Grammar

1 Click on **Tools**, or press **Alt+T**.

2 Click on **Grammatik**, or press **G**.

3 Select options if desired, then click on **Start**, or press **Enter**.

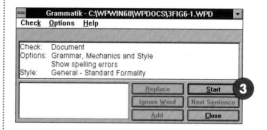

4 If a problem is found, a message appears in the message box. Choose from the option buttons to address the problem and continue the grammar check.

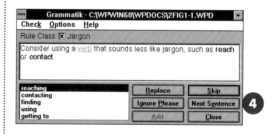

5 When the grammar check is complete, a dialog box will appear to verify the check. Click on **Yes**, or press **Enter**.

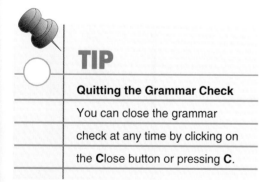

TIP

Quitting the Grammar Check

You can close the grammar

check at any time by clicking on

the **C**lose button or pressing **C**.

USING THE DRAWING PROGRAM

How Does the Drawing Program Work?

WordPerfect for Windows 6.0 comes with a *drawing program* that can be used to add graphics, figures, and even charts to your documents. Similar to other graphics programs, the drawing program has tools to draw with, and extensive options for creating professional-looking designs.

The program uses the mouse pointer to select tools and draw in the drawing window, and various menu commands to edit the drawing. Although one of the best ways to learn about a drawing program is to begin experimenting with the tools, it's also a good idea to read through the documentation that came with your WordPerfect program to learn about the intricate details of this drawing feature.

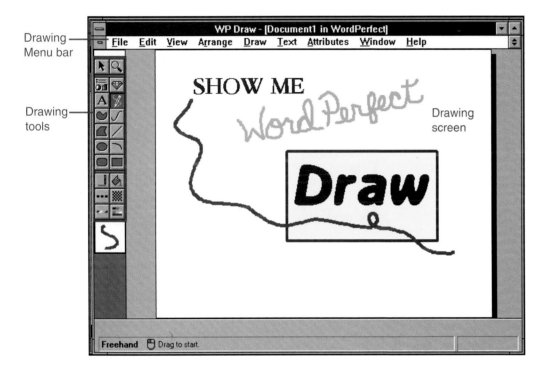

Drawing
Menu bar

Drawing
tools

Drawing
screen

USING THE DRAWING PROGRAM

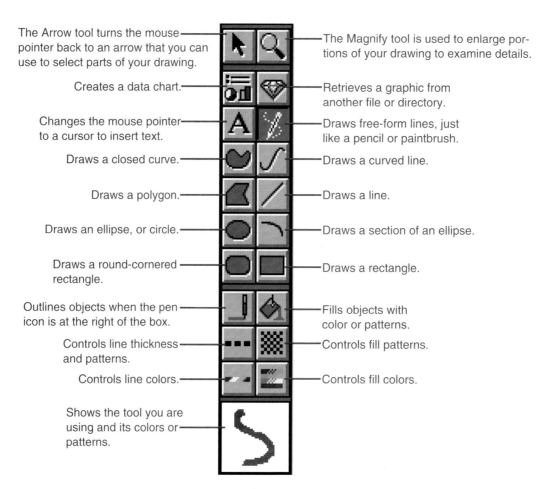

The Arrow tool turns the mouse pointer back to an arrow that you can use to select parts of your drawing.

The Magnify tool is used to enlarge portions of your drawing to examine details.

Creates a data chart.

Retrieves a graphic from another file or directory.

Changes the mouse pointer to a cursor to insert text.

Draws free-form lines, just like a pencil or paintbrush.

Draws a closed curve.

Draws a curved line.

Draws a polygon.

Draws a line.

Draws an ellipse, or circle.

Draws a section of an ellipse.

Draws a round-cornered rectangle.

Draws a rectangle.

Outlines objects when the pen icon is at the right of the box.

Fills objects with color or patterns.

Controls line thickness and patterns.

Controls fill patterns.

Controls line colors.

Controls fill colors.

Shows the tool you are using and its colors or patterns.

TIP

Quick Draw You can also click on the **Draw** button on the Button Bar.

Draw

TIP

More Drawing You can also use the **Chart** feature to access the drawing program and create pie charts, graphs, and other charting figures. To select charts, click on **G**raphics or press **Alt+G**. Then click on Chart or press **R**. You'll also find a **Chart** button on the Button Bar for accessing this feature.

Opening the Drawing Program

1 Click on **G**raphics, or press **Alt+G**.

2 Click on **D**raw, or press **D**.

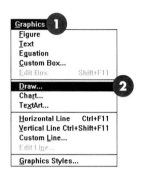

3 Select from the tools and menu options to begin drawing.

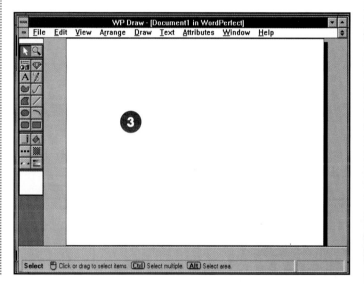

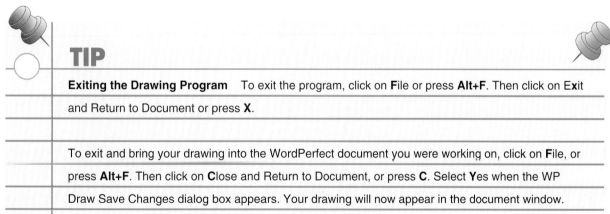

TIP

Exiting the Drawing Program   To exit the program, click on **F**ile or press **Alt+F**. Then click on E**x**it and Return to Document or press **X**.

To exit and bring your drawing into the WordPerfect document you were working on, click on **F**ile, or press **Alt+F**. Then click on **C**lose and Return to Document, or press **C**. Select **Y**es when the WP Draw Save Changes dialog box appears. Your drawing will now appear in the document window.

Enhancing Your Document

GLOSSARY

active document   The document you are currently working on. It will have a highlighted Title bar. When more than one document is opened, only one window can be worked on at a time.

alignment   Positioning of text between the left and right margins. Also known as *justification*.

antonym   A word that means the opposite of another word.

applications   Programs that run on your computer, such as word processors, spreadsheets, databases, and graphics programs.

attributes   Changes made in the look of text, such as making it bolder and larger, or positioning. Also called *formatting*.

cascade   To arrange multiple documents in smaller windows so that they overlap with their title bars visible.

cell   A section in a table where information is typed. Cells usually resemble a box.

click   A light, quick press or tap of the mouse button.

Clipboard   A temporary storage area for text and graphics.

commands   Orders that tell the computer what to do.

context-sensitive   A type of help system that takes you directly to the information pertaining to the task you are trying to perform, without routing you through a topical index.

cursor   A blinking vertical line that indicates where typed characters will appear. Also known as the *insertion point*.

dialog box   A box that appears when the program requires additional information to carry out a command.

directory   Special areas in your computer's hard disk where files are stored.

disk drive   A device that enables the computer to store data on a magnetic disk. (See *floppy disk drive* and *hard drive*.)

documents   Work, such as a letter or a memo, created using a word processing program.

DOS prompt   A set of characters on the left side of the screen, followed by a blinking underline. DOS commands are typed in at the DOS prompt.

double-click   Two quick taps of the mouse button.

drag   To press and hold the mouse button while moving the mouse to a new location.

107

edit   To make changes in your text, or otherwise modify your document.

ellipsis   Three dots following a menu command, which indicate a dialog box will appear when the command is selected.

existing document   A document that has been saved before.

Feature Bar   A special bar of options that appears below the Power Bar when you are working with headers and footers.

file   The storage location of your document on disk when you save it. Files are given unique *file names* that distinguish them from other files.

file extension   An extra name added to a file name that helps determine what kind of file it is, such as .LTR (SMITH.LTR) or .DOC (REPORT.DOC).

floppy disk   A small, portable magnetic disk used to save and store the data created on your computer.

floppy disk drive   A disk drive in your computer that uses floppy disks.

font   A set of characters that has a consistent design.

footer   Text that is repeated at the bottom of every page, or on alternating pages. Footers can include chapter titles, file names, dates, etc.

formatting   Changes made to the look of text, such as making it bolder and larger, or altering its position. Also called *attributes* or *text enhancements*.

Grammatik   A program within WordPerfect for Windows 6.0 that checks your documents for grammatical errors.

hanging indent   An indent with the first line of the text block flush left with the left margin, and the remainder of the text block indented. Hanging indents are typically used with bulleted or numbered lists.

hard disk   A permanent disk drive located inside your computer. Hard drives hold more data than floppy disks.

header   Text that is repeated at the top of every page or alternating pages. Headers can include report titles, company name, dates, etc.

highlight   A black background or bar, surrounding a word or group of words, indicating the text is selected. Once text is highlighted, commands that will affect it can be executed.

I-beam   "Capital I" shape the mouse pointer assumes when it is anywhere inside the text area of your screen.

icon   A small picture or graphic that represents a program, a command, or a piece of information.

indent   To shift a line of text away from the left or right margins.

Insert mode   Adding text without deleting any existing characters. Existing text is shifted to the right of the insertion point as new text is typed.

justification   The positioning of text with respect to a document's left and right margins. Also called *alignment*.

margin   The space between your text and the outer edge of your page.

menu   A list of commands (or other choices) displayed in a drop-down box on your screen.

mouse   A device used to move the cursor or the highlighting around the computer screen, pointing at various program elements to select them.

paragraph   A group of words that is treated as a block of text. Paragraphs can also be single lines, captions, bulleted text, and even blank lines. A paragraph is created by pressing the **Enter** key at the end of a line.

point size   The height of text characters as measured in *points* (one point equals 1/72-inch).

retrieving   To bring a document into your current document window. WordPerfect calls this process *inserting*.

selection bar   The narrow area to the left of the left margin, used to select blocks of text. The mouse pointer becomes an arrow when placed anywhere inside the selection bar.

selection letter   An underlined letter in the menu or command name. Keyboard users can choose the command or menu by holding down the **Alt** key and pressing the underlined selection letter.

shortcut key   A key, or combination of keys, that can be pressed to execute a command without opening menus.

special codes   Formatting codes WordPerfect for Windows 6.0 places within your document to indicate where the formatting begins and ends.

synonym   A word that means the same thing as another word.

tab   A keystroke that moves text to a specified point in your document. Tabs are used to align text.

table   A chart of information arranged in rows and columns.

text block   Any amount of text you want to work with, ranging from a single character to an entire document.

text enhancements   A characteristic (such as italics) applied to text.

Thesaurus   A special program within WordPerfect for Windows 6.0 that allows you to look up synonyms and antonyms.

tile   To arrange multiple document windows into non-overlapping squares on the screen.

Typeover mode   Adding text that takes the place of existing text. Also called *overstrike mode*.

wrapping   Starting the next line of text automatically when the end of a line is reached.

zoom   To magnify a portion of a document.

INSTALLING WORDPERFECT FOR WINDOWS 6.0

Before you can use WordPerfect for Windows 6.0, you must first install the program on your computer. This section is for those of you who have not yet installed the program.

You will need to have ready all the diskettes that came with the WordPerfect for Windows 6.0 package. These diskettes may be the 3 1/2-inch or 5 1/4-inch size, and are labeled "Install 1," "Program 1," "Program 2," and so on.

Installation Steps

1 Turn on your computer and start Windows.

2 Insert the diskette labeled **Install 1** into your computer's diskette drive.

3 At the Windows Program Manager screen, click on **File** or press **Alt+F** to display the **File** menu.

4 Click on **Run**, or press **R** to display the Run dialog box.

5 In the Command Line text box, type **a:install** (if you're using the A drive), or **b:install** (if you're using the B drive). Then click on **OK** or press **Enter**.

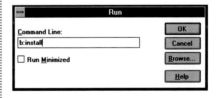

6 The installation program displays the Registration Information dialog box. Type in your name and program license number, then click on Continue or press **Enter**.

7 Choose an installation option from the Installation Type dialog box. Click on the appropriate button, or press the selection letter. *Note: You can install a minimum setup that only takes up 14MB if you're low on space.*

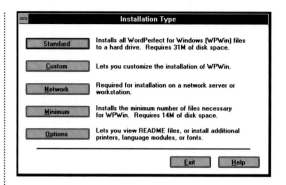

8 The next dialog box to appear on your screen is the Select Drive box. Select the disk drive on which you want to install WordPerfect for Windows. Then click on **OK** or press **Enter**.

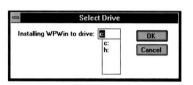

9 The Install Files dialog box will appear, and begin copying the WordPerfect for Windows program files onto your designated drive.

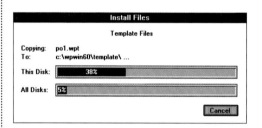

10 Follow the instructions that appear on-screen, changing diskettes when prompted.

11 When the installation is complete, follow the instructions to

return to the Program Manager screen. WordPerfect for Windows 6.0 is ready to go!

Index

115

L

Layout menu commands
    Font, 74-75
    Header/Footer, 91-93
    Justification, 88-89
    Line
        Spacing, 90
        Tab Set, 82-83
    Margins, 80-81
    Paragraph Indent, 86
leader dots, 82
left tabs, 82
left-aligned text, 87
Line command (Layout menu)
    Spacing, 90
    Tab Set, 82-83
line spacing, 90
Line Spacing button, Power Bar, 90
Line Spacing dialog box, 90
lines, blank, 34
list boxes, 18-19

M

margins, 79-81, 109
Margins command (Layout menu), 80-81
Margins dialog box, 80-81
Maximize button, 15
memory, RAM (random-access memory), 7
menu bar, 2, 15-16
    Draw program, 103
menus, 109
    selecting commands, 16-17
messages, Bad command or file-name, 12
Minimize button, 15
modes
    Insert, 109
        versus Typeover, 38-39
    Select, 45
    Typeover, 110
monitors, 6
mouse, 6, 109
    clicking, 107
    double-clicking, 107
        selecting words, 43
    dragging, 107
    operations, 8
    quadruple-clicking (selecting paragraphs), 43

triple-clicking (selecting sentences), 43
mouse pointer, 14, 36-37
    I-beam, 108
moving
    Button Bar, 23
    tab stops, 84
    text, 50-52
        between documents, 69
multiple documents, 67-69

N

naming files, 56-57
New command (File menu), 34
New Document button, Power Bar, 34

O

Open command (File menu), 59-60
Open File dialog box, 59-60
opening documents, 59-60
option buttons, 18-19
Overstrike mode, 38-39

P

Page Break command (Insert menu), 35
page breaks, 35
Page Zoom Full button, Power Bar, 66
paired codes, 78
Paragraph Indent command (Layout menu), 86
paragraphs, 32-33, 109
    selecting, 44
        quadruple-clicking, 43
Paste button, Power Bar, 52
Paste command (Edit menu), 51-52, 54-55
pasting text, 50-52
point sizes, 74, 109
pointing, 8
ports, 7
Power Bar, 15, 21
    Bold Font button, 76
    buttons, 22
    Copy button, 54
    Cut button, 52
    Font Face button, 76
    Font Size button, 76
    Grammatik tool button, 101

    Italic Font button, 76
    Justify button, 88-89
    Line Spacing button, 90
    New Document button, 34
    Page Zoom Full button, 66
    Paste button, 52
    Print button, 71
    Save button, 58
    Speller tool button, 96-97
    Tab Set button, 83
    Thesaurus tool button, 100
    Underline Font button, 76
    Zoom button, 66
Power Bar command (View menu), 21
Preferences command (File menu), 23
previewing documents by zooming, 65-66
Print button, Power Bar, 71
Print command (File menu), 70-71
Print dialog box, 70-71
Printer Driver dialog box, 112
printers, selecting, 70
printing documents, 70-71
program group windows, 13
Program Manager, 12
    Run command (File menu), 111
    screen, 13
programs, *see* applications
pull-down menus, 16

Q

quadruple-clicking (selecting paragraphs), 43
QuickMenu, Ruler Bar, 79, 84

R

RAM (random-access memory), 7
Registration Information dialog box, 111
Replace command (Edit menu), 62, 64
replacing text, 62, 64
    existing, with new text, 47
Restore button, 15
restoring
    deleted text, 48
    windows, 15
retrieving, 109
returns, 33

Index

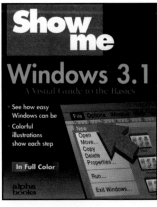